WHAT DID HE SAY?

WHAT DID HE SAY?

Recognizing God's Voice Amidst the
Turmoil of Life

KAYE ALLENE ALLEN

Xulon Press

Xulon Press
555 Winderley Pl, Suite 225
Maitland, FL 32751
407.339.4217
www.xulonpress.com

INTRODUCTION

"I will stand at my guard post and station myself on the ramparts. I will watch to see what He will say to me, and how I should answer when corrected."
Habakkuk 2:1

TODAY, YOU ARE embarking on a journey alongside me. This journey will take us to the truth of God's Word and offer practical guidance on how to receive a personal message from God through His Word.

Such guidance has been a significant part of my life story. The purpose behind writing this book is to empower you, enabling you to learn what God conveys specifically about you in His Word. To guide, lead, and direct you personally.

Early in my life, I learned a transformative lesson that has consistently proven invaluable in every situation and circumstance along my journey, and never failed me in any situation or circumstance: to read, study, and obediently follow when God speaks through His Word. This lesson has served as a steadfast beacon during the darkest of times. It has directed me when I felt lost and needed guidance when answers seemed elusive. It's guided me through sunshine and shadows alike.

A scripture from the Book of Habakkuk provides insight into what is required to receive God's guidance:

> *"I will stand at my guard post and station myself on the ramparts. I will watch to see what He will say to me, and how I should answer when corrected."*
> *Habakkuk 2:1*

God's desire is to engage and communicate with each of us personally. He longs to impart intimate details into our lives for the purpose of leading, correcting, directing, instructing, and guiding us. But we must stand at attention. To "watch and see" what He will say. This goes beyond mere listening. We must actively look and pay attention. When we look, we heighten our awareness, allowing us to anticipate and see what we can't always hear.

The concept of "watching to see" involves the function of the eye gate, where "what He will say to me" enters our minds visually. The written Word serves as one source of "what we see" and through this God communicates. By this means, God will "say," He will speak. He provides answers to the questions we pose, offers guidance for pressing decisions, imparts the encouragement we require, and reveals a path forward when we are lost or confused, unsure of what to do or where to go.

This mirrors the story of David in 1 Samuel 30, where, upon returning to the village of Ziklag from war, he found the village in ruins and all the women and children kidnapped. At that dire moment, even his own men contemplated stoning him to death. In this challenging situation, David somehow found a way to encourage himself in the Lord, and as a result, God spoke to him and led him forward.

Steps

The journey of learning to recognize God's voice and discern His guidance is a gradual process. Learning to identify his leadings and guidance became a series of steps for me. Hearing specific instructions, and finding answers, is not something learned overnight. It's akin to how children learn to speak and comprehend language over time. It's a lifetime of learning. A process. A journey of thousands of little steps. God leads us in steps, not in leaps and bounds.

My journey of faith started young. I was raised in a Christian home and learned at a young age to study what God had to say. I learned the importance of walking in obedience to God's truths. This practice brought me into a more intimate relationship with God. Slowly it became easier to recognize His direction day to day as He taught, reproved, corrected, and trained me in right living.

My mother provided the example for me to pursue this wonderful life pathway. Admittedly, this example didn't appear valuable to me as a teenager. However, maturity caused me to appreciate her words of wisdom. Her words found lodging in my mind and heart. Eventually, the truth of two scriptures from 2 Timothy became a significant part of my life.

What Did He Say?

"Study to show thyself approved unto God a workman that needs not be ashamed, rightly dividing the word of truth." 2 Timothy 2:15

"All Scripture is breathed out by God and is profitable for teaching, for reproof, for correction, and for training in righteousness." 2 Timothy 3:16

My siblings and I were not privileged to have meaningful conversations about life with our parents. We considered "conversations" held to be awkward and somewhat frustrating. Once I attempted to strike up a dialogue about dating with my mother. As was more normal than not, my mother didn't address the question because her response was distant and off-topic. She quoted a scripture that she felt could be utilized to provide A LESSON she wanted to teach me on the subject without addressing my concern and questions.

Invaluable Lessons

What Did He Say?

"Today I have set before you life and death, a blessing and a curse, so choose life, in order that you may live, you and your descendants." Deuteronomy 30:19

CHAPTER 1

"For the words which You gave Me I have given to them; and they received them and truly understood that I came forth from You, and they believed that You sent Me." John 17:8

GOD HAS CONSISTENTLY revealed Himself as a communicator since the dawn of time, as evident in the opening verses of the Bible. Genesis 1:3 declares, "God said, 'Let there be light,' and it was so!" The entire account of creation depicted in Genesis is a testament to God's communication, as He spoke words into the void. Following each divine declaration, the words "And it was so" resound, underscoring that God's spoken word never returns empty.

God's crowning achievement in creation was humanity, the final act and the only aspect of creation made in His image. God had much more to convey about His magnum opus than any other element of creation. He bestowed freedom, abundance, dominion, and promise upon humanity, along with a multitude of blessings. Amidst this bountiful provision, He included one important caution:

> **"You may eat freely from all the trees of the garden, but do not eat from the tree of the knowledge of good and evil, for on the day you eat from it, you will surely die!"**

Listening and Understanding

What Did He Say?

"Let the person who has ears, listen!" The disciples asked him, "Why do you use stories as illustrations when you speak to people?" Matthew 13:9-10

Jesus repeatedly emphasized the word "Listen" in His interactions with others. In Matthew 13, Jesus imparts vital lessons to a crowd through stories and begins His teaching with a resounding "Listen!" He then proceeds to share a parable about a farmer sowing seeds. Some seeds fell along the roadside and were devoured by birds, while others landed on rocky ground, sprouted quickly, but withered away due to shallow soil and inadequate roots. Some seeds were choked by thorn bushes, while others flourished in good soil, yielding abundant grain. Jesus concludes the story with a profound insight and challenge: *"Those who understand ... will be given more knowledge, and they will excel in understanding them."* Matthew 13:12

Jesus informs that the remarkable benefit of attentive listening is the acquisition of greater knowledge and the ability to excel in understanding. This particular scene confused the twelve disciples.

Prompting one of them to ask, "Why do you use stories when you talk to the people? Jesus seized this opportunity to address the crucial concepts of hearing, listening and understanding. *"This is why I speak to them this way. They see, but they're blind. They <u>hear</u>, but they don't <u>listen</u>. They don't even try to <u>understand</u>. So, they make Isaiah's prophecy come true:*

He explained, *"I speak to them in parables because they see but remain blind; they hear but do not truly listen, and they make no effort to understand. In this way, they fulfill Isaiah's prophecy:"*

> *'You will <u>hear</u> clearly but never <u>understand</u>.*
> *You will see clearly but never comprehend.*
> *These people have become <u>close-minded and hard of hearing</u>.*
> *They have shut their eyes so that their eyes never see.*
> *Their ears never <u>hear</u>. Their minds never <u>understand</u>.*
> *And they never return to me for healing!'*

> *"Listen to what the story about the farmer means. Someone hears the word about the kingdom but doesn't understand it. The evil one comes at once and snatches away what was planted in him. This is what the seed planted along the road illustrates. The seed planted on rocky ground is the person who hears the word and accepts it at once with joy. Since he doesn't have any roots, he lasts only a little while. When suffering or persecution comes along because of the word, he immediately falls from faith. The seed planted among thorn bushes is another person who hears the word. But the worries of life and the deceitful pleasures of riches choke the word so that it can't produce anything. But the seed planted on*

3

good ground is the person who hears and understands the word. This type produces crops. They produce one hundred, sixty, or thirty times as much as was planted." Matthew 13:18 - 23

"And with many other words, he (Peter) solemnly testified and kept on exhorting them, saying, 'Be saved from this perverse generation!" vs. 41 "So then, those who had received his word were baptized; and there were added that day about 3,000 souls." Acts 2:40

CHAPTER 2

EACH PERSON POSSESSES a unique calling in life, and this calling remains impervious to the limitations imposed by one's past, heritage, or current circumstances. The voices that surround us—whether they originate from within ourselves, others, or even our adversaries—hold no power to determine how we fulfill that calling unless we willingly grant them authority and credibility. In I Samuel 23:2 King David needed an answer from God.

> *"So, David inquired of the Lord, saying, "Shall I go and attack these Philistines? And the Lord said to David, "Go and attack the Philistines, and deliver Keilah.* I Samuel 23:2

> *"Behold, we are afraid here in Judah. How much more than if we go to Keilah against the ranks of the Philistines? Then David inquired of the Lord once more. And the Lord answered him and said, 'Arise, go down to Keilah, for I will give the Philistines into your hand.'"* I Samuel 23:2-4

"So, David saved the inhabitants of Keilah." I Samuel 23:5b

What Did He Say?

"The steps of a man are established by the Lord; and He delights in his way." Psalm 37:23

"Father, if you are willing, please take this cup of suffering away from me. Yet I want your will, not mine. Then an angel from heaven appeared and strengthened him." Luke 22:43

Notice a significant statement in Luke 22:43: **"Then an angel from heaven appeared and strengthened him."** The strength came after the surrender.

Your unique purpose is likely to revolve around a similar central theme and contain the same focus. Regardless of what God calls you to do, it will invariably align with God's overarching plan for your life and may entail interactions with other individuals. It's essential to recognize that God's will for our lives often extends beyond our personal experiences and should not be viewed through a narrow perspective, a myopic lens. The broader scope of His will reaches out to impact others and potentially leaves a lasting legacy for generations to come, as illustrated by the examples of David and Jesus. To see God's will fulfilled, surrender is a vital component in the journey.

God taught me an important lesson on surrender in the early days of my marriage. At that time, my husband and I were parents to three young children—two boys in elementary school and an infant daughter. Before our youngest child's birth, I had been working outside the home. However, after her arrival, I made the decision to become a stay-at-home mom.

During this phase of my life, I had a cute little car, a charming Navy Blue Volkswagen Fastback. After dropping off my boys at school, I found myself with lots of free time. So, I would load my baby girl into the car, and off we sped to do whatever I pleased until around 3:00 p.m. when the boys returned from school. Gradually, I realized I was spending much of my time unproductively and it wasn't God's plan for me to waste so much time and energy.

One morning in church, I felt God ask me to sell my car. I sensed God was calling me to do so because He wanted me to use some of those hours for a greater purpose. He was challenging me to spend more time with Him in prayer and His Word. This would be far more productive than running around the Seattle area all day. So, that afternoon I told my husband about what I believed God was calling me to do. My husband agreed and told me to sell the car. I investigated the Blue Book price for my little car and decided to sell it for that price.

The following Sunday, a young couple approached me at church and said they were looking to buy a car like mine and wondered if it was for sale. I was so surprised! I told them it was for sale and quoted the Blue Book price and they bought my car.

That moment was a turning point in my life. I had committed to surrendering some of my personal time to God. To accomplish that, I needed to surrender my vehicle. And once I was obedient to what God had spoken to my heart, I found peace and fulfillment and began to identify my purpose and calling. It was during that season I learned to love God's Word and see it as a manual for life. I learned to identify and hear His voice and walk in obedience to His Word.

What Did He Say?

"Then the Lord God said, 'It is not good for the man to be alone; I will make him a <u>helper suitable for him.</u>" Genesis 2:18

"For this cause a man shall leave his father and his mother and shall cleave to his wife; and they shall become one flesh." Genesis 2:24

What Did He Say?

"For I know the plans I have for you says the Lord, plans to prosper you and not to harm you to give you a future and a hope." Jeremiah 29:11

"I will stand at my guard post and station myself on the ramparts. I will watch to see what He will say to me, and how I should answer when corrected." Habakkuk 2:

CHAPTER 3

"But . . . lend, expecting nothing in return, and your reward will be great." Luke 6:35

DISCOVERING ANSWERS TO life's practical questions can be difficult. Where should I attend school? Whom should I marry? Where is the best place to live? Which job should I pursue? What will be the ultimate standard of truth in my life? Every decision we make has consequences, not just for ourselves but also for future generations. No answers or choices are insignificant.

The first step toward discovering answers to life's questions based on truth is a sincere desire to know them. For those who seek answers, God offers a pathway illuminated by the truth of His Word.

"Thy word is a lamp unto my feet, and a light unto my path." Psalm 119:105

"You shall know the truth and the truth will set you free." John 8:32

> *"His divine power has given us everything required for life and godliness through the knowledge of Him who called us by His own glory and goodness."* 2 Peter 1:3

All questions related to life and godliness can be answered through the knowledge of Him, Jesus, who is the way, the truth, and the life. This is God's provision for finding answers to life's questions. However, what is our part in discovering the truth concerning the personal situations we face?

> *"Trust in the Lord with all thy heart and lean not on your own understanding. In all your ways acknowledge Him and He shall make your path straight."* Proverbs 3:5 – 6

As a young mother, discovering this truth transformed my life. The Bible became a dependable source for me to find answers to life's questions, including answers to my questions for my personal life. This realization came as I continued to read a portion from the Bible each day, eventually leading me to read through the entire Bible.

On one occasion, I had a question that troubled me, and I needed to find an answer. While the answer may have seemed simple at the time, it taught me a valuable life lesson that has protected me from making mistakes on more significant issues I've faced across the years.

My husband, Harley, and I, along with our two young boys, moved into a newly constructed neighborhood comprising five homes, each on about three-quarters of an acre of land. We, along with the neighboring couples, spent a lot of time landscaping our large yards. Friendships developed with our new neighbors. We became good friends, spending time together socially.

Periodically, my neighbor who lived closest to me began "borrowing" items from me. At first, it was just a cup of sugar or a loaf of bread, which I didn't mind. However, as time went by, I discovered that her definition of "borrowing" differed from mine. I believed that borrowing meant returning what had been borrowed, whereas to my neighbor, borrowing meant keeping whatever she was given. This trend continued until she started "borrowing" kitchen utensils and small appliances, never returning anything she took. As a result, our relationship began to suffer, and I found myself praying to God for guidance.

As usual, I reached for my Bible and opened it to the next section of the Book of Luke, where I had left off the day before. I wondered what God's word would say, and whether it would provide me with an answer to my problem.

What Did He Say?

"But . . . lend, hoping for nothing in return and your reward will be great." Luke 6:35.

I was astounded by the speed and clarity of the answer God had provided me that morning. It was remarkable how precisely it addressed my question. And I found it right there in the pages of the Bible. Armed with this knowledge, I felt empowered to make a wise decision regarding my relationship with my neighbor, and I resolved to follow the Scripture's guidance.

It's important to note that the truth God revealed to me that morning went beyond the issue of a cup of sugar, a loaf of bread, or a small appliance. As I continued to grow in my faith and deepen my understanding of scripture, I realized that the same principle applied to other situations, such as when I loaned money to a family member for expensive dental work, only for it not to be repaid. This presented a new challenge, and I had to ask myself what my next course of action should be. What should I do? Is this a principle that is to be lived out in every circumstance?

> *"But ... lend hoping for nothing in return and your reward will be great."* Luke 6:35

The lesson I learned as a young wife and mother still resonates with me today, even as a great-grandmother. This truth from God's Word serves as a guiding light as I navigate life's decisions and challenges.

When faced with God's message, it's easy to respond by saying, "That's not fair." However, it's essential to recognize that there's a significant difference between receiving a cup of sugar, which is trivial, and being burdened with an expensive dental bill. Instead of striving for fairness here on earth, it's vital to focus on our eternal reward in heaven. Why should I consider, or desire fairness, to be a measuring stick in this life when it comes to being obedient to what God asks me to do or give? Does He not have my best interests in mind?

God has promised us eternal rewards. Often, we miss, or forget about this entire aspect of life that is to come with a myopic view of the present. Why should fairness be my focus or goal when I could be looking forward to eternal rewards? Listen to what God says at the end of verse 35:

> *". . .and your reward in heaven will be great."*

So, when we consider our choices, it's crucial to keep this in mind. Our reward in heaven is everlasting, so it's more valuable than any earthly reward we might seek. This realization helps us prioritize our decisions and choose what is ultimately beneficial for our eternal reward.

His Thoughts Are Not Our Thoughts

"For my thoughts are not your thoughts, neither are your ways my ways," declares the LORD. "As the heavens are higher than the earth, so are my ways higher than your ways and my thoughts than your thoughts. Isaiah 55:8–9

God's ways are higher than our ways. It can be exciting and worthwhile to wait for the eternal reward that God has prepared for us, knowing that His plans and ways are beyond our own understanding. This scripture reminds us to trust in His wisdom and not solely rely on our own human reasoning when seeking answers from His Word.

Another scripture to keep in mind when seeking answers in the Word of God that may challenge our way of thinking or our own understanding is 2 Corinthians 4:18:

"So, we fix our eyes not on what is seen, but on what is unseen. For the things which are seen, are temporal; but the things which are not seen, are eternal."

This scripture serves as a reminder to keep our focus on the rewards in heaven rather than the troubles we face in the present moment. As it is written:

"We don't look at the troubles we can see now; rather, we fix our gaze on things that cannot be seen, i.e., the rewards in heaven. For the things we see now will soon be gone, but the things we cannot see will last forever." (2 Corinthians 4:18)

When we come across answers in the scriptures that challenge our understanding, it is important to acknowledge that we cannot fully comprehend God's ways or thoughts. From our limited earthly perspective, it may even seem unfair. However, we can trust that God's ways are higher than our ways and that He has a greater plan that we may not fully grasp.

What Did He Say?

"O the depth of the riches both of the wisdom and knowledge of God! How unsearchable are His judgments, and His ways past finding out!" Romans 11:33

Our limited human minds cannot comprehend the vastness of God's ways. Therefore, why would we settle for what is merely fair when we can receive rewards from the boundless riches of God? As the scripture says, "Lend, hoping for nothing in return, and your reward will be great." So, what should we do? We have a choice to make:

1. Acknowledge that God's ways are beyond our understanding.
2. Keep our focus on the eternal reward promised by God, rather than the temporary things we can see.
3. Obey His Word, even when we don't fully grasp the reasons behind it.

CHAPTER 4

"Behold, I am coming quickly, and My reward is with Me, to render to every man according to what he has done." (Revelation 22:12)

LIFE PRESENTS COUNTLESS choices every day. Most daily decisions we make are related to time and energy, how we utilize these resources. We're also faced with moral choices daily: Our actions, both in public and when no one is watching, our interactions with others, whether they are strangers or acquaintances, all reflect the vast array of choices we make in our lives. Among the most profound lessons we can acquire is the ability to carefully assess our decisions using two critical considerations:

1. How will I allocate my time, skills, words, and financial resources?
2. Will these investments contribute to something with lasting significance, or will they merely serve the transient needs of today, vanishing tomorrow?

The Bible provides an illustrative example of this principle in the Garden of Eden, at the beginning of God's relationship with humanity. God gave Adam and Eve specific instructions and presented them with a choice: to eat from the tree of the knowledge of good and evil or not. God explained the consequences of their actions, warning if they ate from the tree they would surely die. However, Satan tempted them with a lie, claiming they would become like God and not die. Adam and Eve were lured by the temporary benefits of forbidden fruit, desiring to know evil despite already knowing "good." They believed Satan's deception and ate the fruit. The consequences were immediate and severe. Their relationship with God was broken, and they were filled with fear and shame. They became afraid of God. They attempted to hide from him. They experienced spiritual death, losing their purity and sinlessness. Their intimate relationship with God was destroyed. Most significantly, they were now susceptible to eternal death.

As with so much negativity in people's lives, this nightmarish scene could have been avoided. God had already promised Adam unimaginable blessing. Let's not forget what God said to Adam before He created Eve:

> *"The Lord God commanded the human, 'Eat your fill from all of the garden's trees; but don't eat from the tree of the knowledge of good and evil, because on the day you eat from it you will die!'"* (Genesis 2:16 & 17)

The expression "eat your fill" conveys a profound sense of contentment and fulfillment rooted in obedience to God. His provision consistently proves sufficient to satisfy our needs. However, in a cunning move, Satan endeavored to persuade Eve that God's offering was inadequate and incapable of meeting her desires. He insinuated that God was withholding something, promising genuine satisfaction, and asserted that the forbidden fruit would not result in the death God had warned of. Instead, he claimed it would open her eyes to the knowledge of good and evil, making her god-like. This deceptive tactic, one of Satan's oldest tricks, has historically led people down paths they never anticipated. Instead of discovering fulfillment, individuals often encounter emptiness and unfulfilled promises. It's a tragic journey mirrored by countless others throughout history, just as Eve once walked.

Unintended Consequences of Choices

It's worth emphasizing that our choices always have consequences. Not only for ourselves, but for the lives of others in our circle, and for future generations as well. The instruction from God's word is clear:

"I call heaven and earth to testify against you today! I've set life and death before you today: both blessings and curses. Choose life, that it may be well with you – you and your children." (Deuteronomy 30:19)

What Did He Say?

"Choose life in order that you may live, you and your descendants!" (Deuteronomy 30:19)

"The heart of man plans his way, but the Lord establishes his steps." (Proverbs 16:9)

Our choices always have consequences, and it's important to remember that decisions determine our outcomes. What choices will you make in your life, in times of dilemma, temptation, trial, failure, success, happiness, and doubt? The Book of Acts includes an extraordinary passage of scripture that addresses the concepts of choice, understanding, and knowledge.

> *"Lord, are you going to restore the kingdom to Israel now? Jesus replied, "It isn't for you to know the times or seasons that the Father has set by his own authority. Rather, you will receive power when the Holy Spirit has come upon you, and you will be my witnesses in Jerusalem, in all Judea and Samaria, and to the end of the earth. It's not for you to know the times and seasons but this is what I want you to know. You will receive power when the Holy Spirit has come upon you for the purpose of being my witnesses."* (Acts 1:6-8)

When confronted with the decision between knowledge and power, what do we prioritize? Frequently, we become fixated on knowing the timing of events or when we will receive answers to our prayers. How often do we inquire about "when"? How frequently do we yearn for knowledge? When will my family embrace and live for you? When will we retire? However, God doesn't always intend for us to know "when." Instead, He desires us to realize that we possess the power to live each day through Christ within us, irrespective of what we know or do not know. We have the power to place our trust in God, exercise faith, and practice self-denial.

In the book of Ecclesiastes, Chapter Three, God imparts valuable wisdom regarding the timing of events that is worth embracing.

These circumstances are anticipated in our lives, and we should not be taken aback when they transpire. Nonetheless, it's crucial to recognize that each of these occurrences serves a distinct purpose. By submitting ourselves to God, we can navigate these situations with the strength of Christ dwelling within us. As the scripture says, "There is a time for everything:"

1   There is a time for everything, and a season for every activity under the heavens:

2   A time to be born and a time to die, a time to plant and a time to uproot,

3   A time to kill and a time to heal, a time to tear down and a time to build,

4   A time to weep and a time to laugh, a time to mourn and a time to dance,

5   A time to scatter stones and a time to gather them, a time to embrace and a time to refrain from embracing,

6   A time to search and a time to give up, a time to keep and a time to throw away,

7   A time to tear and a time to mend, a time to be silent and a time to speak,

8   A time to love and a time to hate, a time for war and a time for peace. (Ecclesiastes 3:1-8)

CHAPTER 5

"Don't do anything for selfish purposes, but with humility think of others as better than yourselves. Instead of each person watching out for their own good, watch out for what is better for others. Adopt the attitude that was in Christ Jesus. . ."
(Philippians 2:3 – 5)

LIFE IS PRIMARILY defined by relationships, extending into nearly every aspect of our existence: our connection with God, family, friends, co-workers, neighbors, teammates, acquaintances, professionals, advisors, and counselors, among others. The list is boundless.

To nurture strong relationships, we must redirect our focus away from self-centered desires towards embracing humility and genuine concern for others. There exists a profound connection between living for oneself and the concept of dying to oneself in the context of our relationships.

Arguably, nothing impacts our emotional well-being more significantly than our interactions with others. People can bring us both immense joy and profound sorrow, and their words and actions can wield a substantial emotional influence over us, just as their silence can.

Our emotional reactions often hinge on our preconceived expectations regarding how others should behave or respond to us. When these expectations are met, we might experience elation, but when they remain unfulfilled, disappointment, fear, and even depression can set in. It's crucial to acknowledge that our emotions are directly shaped by the people in our lives.

What Did He Say?

"You were bought and paid for. Don't become slaves of people." I Cor: 7:23

Refrain from letting the opinions or actions of others exert control over you. The term "slave" connotes being under the ownership of someone else. When we permit others to influence our thoughts and behaviors, they effectively gain power over us.

According to scripture, we are not meant to be enslaved by people. Instead, we should surrender ourselves to Jesus as our ultimate guide and master. He made the ultimate sacrifice to redeem us, so our lives should be devoted to pleasing Him above all else. Our commitment should be to serve Him, regardless of how others may treat us or what they may say. By becoming devoted to the one who paid the ultimate price for our salvation, we liberate ourselves from the tyranny of self. The book of Philippians explores this concept in greater depth:

"Adopt the attitude that was in Christ Jesus; Though he was in the form of God, he did not consider being

equal with God something to exploit. But emp-
tied himself by taking the form of a slave and by
becoming like human beings. When he found him-
self in the form of a human, he humbled himself by
becoming obedient to the point of death, even death
on a cross." (Philippians 2: 5 – 8)

Jesus serves as the prime example of a life marked by self-denial, as reflected in the phrase "humbled himself." This act of humility is a deliberate choice, demanding one to actively suppress selfish desires. Nonetheless, it contradicts our inherent sinful inclinations, rendering it one of the most formidable lessons to grasp. Consistent practice and unwavering dedication are essential, especially concerning our emotions. The act of "dying to self" requires an unwavering focus and commitment on a daily basis, particularly when it comes to managing our emotional life. We must engage in this daily practice of self-denial, especially in the realm of our emotions.

Jesus' genuine strength wasn't showcased in his capacity to instruct and guide massive gatherings; instead, it was evident in his readiness to surrender his own desires and endure suffering, even to the extent of facing death. Fulfilling our own calling undoubtedly demands strength, yet it may be an even more formidable task to summon the strength to embrace humility and let go of our self-importance.

The choice to humble ourselves bears substantial influence on our emotional well-being, with the potential to either fortify or weaken us. Consequently, it is unquestionably worthwhile to consciously opt for humility in any situation where we encounter emotional challenges from others in our lives.

The Book of Luke provides an outstanding portrayal of a person who has humbled oneself and died to selfish and self-serving desires. Luke 6:27-45, provides characteristics of such an individual:

> *Love your enemies.*
> *Do good to those who hate you.*
> *Bless those who curse you.*
> *Pray for those who mistreat you.*
> *If someone slaps you on the cheek, offer the other one as well.*
> *If someone takes your coat, don't withhold our shirt either. Give to everyone who asks and don't demand your things back from those who take them. Treat people in the same way that you want them to treat you.*
> *If you love those who love you, why should you be commended? Even sinners love those who love them. If you do good to those who do good to you, why should you be commended? Even sinners do that. If you lend to those from whom you expect repayment, why should you be commended? Even sinners lend to sinners expecting to be paid back in full. Instead, love your enemies, do good and lend expecting nothing in return. If you do, you will have a great reward. You will be acting the way children of the Most High act, for he is kind to ungrateful and wicked people. Be compassionate just as your Father is compassionate. Don't judge, and you won't be judged. Don't condemn and you won't be condemned. Forgive, and you will be forgiven. Give, and it will be given to you. A good portion – packed*

down, firmly shaken, and overflowing – will fall into your lap. The portion you give will determine the portion you receive in return.

CHAPTER 6

"Don't be afraid, go on believing and she will be alright." Luke 8:50 (*Philipps Translation*)

PARENTS OF PRODIGAL children are not an uncommon sight in our society. Young people, often lured by drugs and the allure of casual sex with multiple partners, frequently rebel against the constraints of their parents' guidance. In the 1980s, this became a tragic reality for our family while we served a church as pastors.

Our daughter began experimenting with drugs and would often leave the home at night, occasionally disappearing for days on end, leaving us in a state of constant worry. Despite our efforts to find her and bring her home, she continued down a destructive path. Our attempts to help her proved fruitless and were unproductive.

One morning, as our second son and I were leaving for college, we received a call from the police. They informed us that our daughter was in custody and requested our presence at the police station. This was yet another painful moment in our family's struggle with our daughter's choices.

At the time, our son had requested my presence in his algebra class, admitting that he could not pass without my help. That morning, I was faced with a difficult decision - should I go to the police station or to the algebra class?

It was at that moment that I received a mental picture from God: a pie chart divided into sections, each representing a different aspect of my life. Three of the sections were dedicated to my children, another to my husband, and others to my teaching ministry and my role as a pastor's wife.

The pie chart was a powerful message from God, reminding me that my daughter was just one piece of my life, and there were other important pieces as well. I felt reassured that I should attend the algebra class. Thus, my son and I went to his school. My husband went to the police station with our daughter, while I accompanied our son to the class.

However, our daughter's troubles continued, and she ran away from home soon after the event, traveling from Washington to California with a rough crowd. This was a terrifying experience for me, as I felt waves of fear wash over me for the first time in my life. This was more than mental or emotional. It was a foreboding physical sensation too. In tears, I reached for my Bible and opened it to the book of Luke, where I had been reading. It was then that I heard God speak to my heart that morning.

What Did He Say?

Jesus spoke a powerful word to me that has stayed with me since that day. The words I read that morning were these:

"Don't be afraid, go on believing and she will be alright." Luke 8:50

Incredibly, I turned directly to that page in Scripture that morning. God spoke loud and clear: "Don't be afraid, Kaye. This is what I want you to do - go on believing." He then gave me a wonderful promise that our daughter would be alright. It was clear that I had my part to play, which was to keep believing, while God had His part to play, which was to watch over her and ensure that she would be alright though she lived in blatant disobedience to Him and us. Similar to the story of the younger brother in the Parable of the Prodigal son. The father kept on about his business believing that God would steer him home. And God protected the prodigal during his worldly wanderings.

With this message, I knew exactly what I needed to do and what God would do. I held onto my faith and trust in Him, knowing that He would fulfill His promise and make sure our daughter would be alright.

Faith and Belief Can Lead to Dark Times

During this time, my husband, two sons, and I were living in Spokane, Washington when we received a phone call from Capital Christian Center in Sacramento, California. It had been almost two years since we last heard from our daughter. The church informed us she had shown up there seeking help as she was six months pregnant. We had served on staff at that church when she was younger, so we had relationships with the staff, and they took a personal interest in this dark situation.

The pastor suggested that we fly down to Sacramento to have a meeting with our daughter and some members of the church staff. Without hesitation, we made arrangements to travel to Sacramento. After meeting with the staff and our daughter, they recommended that she choose between two different ministries that offered care for unwed, pregnant girls. Alternatively, she could choose to come back home with us. She spent the night with the youth pastor and his family and contacted us the next morning to inform us that she wanted to come home.

Upon her return to Spokane, we connected our daughter with a local Pregnancy Center where she could receive counseling to decide about her future and that of her baby. She was presented with options of keeping the baby or putting the baby up for adoption.

As I prayed for her, I asked God to guide her in making the best decision for herself and the baby. He brought to my mind the story of Moses and how his mother, Jocabed, made a difficult but wise decision for his life. Despite the Pharaoh's edict that all boy babies be thrown into the Nile River to be put to death, Jocabed placed Moses in a basket lined with tar and set him in the river, where he was discovered by the Pharaoh's daughter. The baby was "adopted" by the princess and Moses was raised in the Pharaoh's palace.

God used Jocabed's act of sacrifice, as it ultimately prepared Moses to lead the children of Israel out of 400 years of bondage in Egypt. One woman's act of selfless sacrifice allowed the nation of Israel to reach the promised land. Through this story, God spoke to me and impressed upon me that adoption was the best choice for the baby. I prayed that our daughter would be able to hear God speak that truth into her heart as she needed to make her own choice. Ultimately, she chose adoption, and her baby boy was raised by a loving, godly family with a background in missionary work. And then, after the baby was born, our daughter ran away again.

Holding On While You Let Go

Perhaps the hardest moments in our spiritual lives are to let go as we fight to hold on. There is nothing natural about letting go. From the moment we entered this world through our mother's womb, we kicked and screamed and clawed because we did not want to let go of the life we knew, the perceived safe place. It's difficult to trust an unseen future, an unseen God. Thus, we wrestle daily to try and control situations in our lives that are often beyond our control. We fret and worry over situations we are powerless to change or control. This is a very difficult place spiritually and emotionally. When our daughter ran away again, our spirits were crushed. What do we do now? The Book of Luke, grants insight into this moral and spiritual dilemma we all face at certain times in our lives.

CHAPTER 7

PARABLES WERE USED by Jesus to teach the people of His day life lessons. These fascinating truths are included in Scripture for our benefit today. In today's world, families find themselves in difficult dilemmas. A war rages on for the minds and hearts of our children. There are millions of voices influencing children today thanks to the explosion of social media. Parents are perplexed about what they should do to help wandering and aimless children. Children that have no sense of faith or who have turned their back completely on God. And for some, to bring their prodigal children back home.

There are some wonderful lessons discovered in a parable found in the fifteenth Chapter of the Book of Luke that are practical and full of wise counsel. The parable famously known as "The Prodigal Son," teaches us about the great love of God and His desire for all His children to be reconciled to Him. It illustrates the joy in heaven when one sinner repents and turns back to God. As parents, we can learn from this parable to never give up on our prodigal children but to continue to pray for them and welcome them back with open arms when they return. We should not be quick to judge or condemn them but rather show them the same love and forgiveness that our Heavenly Father shows us. The parable also teaches us to be responsible with the resources that God has given us, and to use them to bring glory to Him by helping others who are in need.

What Did He Say?

"And He said, a certain man had two sons, and the younger of them said to his father, 'Father, give me the share of the estate that falls to me. And he divided his wealth between them. And not many days later, the younger son gathered everything together and went on a journey into a distant country, and there he squandered his estate with loose living. Now when he had spent everything a severe famine occurred in that country, <u>and he began to be in need.</u> And he went and attached himself to one of the citizens of that country, and he began to be in need. And <u>no one was giving anything to him, but when he came to his senses, he said, "I will get up and go to my father and will say to him, Father, I have sinned against heaven and in your sight.</u>" Luke 15:11-14

This parable is very familiar to my husband and me. I remember what God had said at the commencement of our personal crisis with our daughter: ***"Now don't be afraid, go on believing and she will be alright."*** You may be reading this and are experiencing a similar crisis with your own child. Or perhaps there is another crisis affecting your children, your family, or your own personal life. The parable of "The Prodigal Son" reaches far and wide and offers life lessons and answers for all dilemmas. Here are some lessons from the parable that guided us through many years with our prodigal, and through other spiritual and moral dilemmas we have faced:

1. The Father gave the son his inheritance and sent him on his way regardless of how he felt. This action is a bit counterintuitive to human reaction.

2. The father's actions in the story hold valuable wisdom for us today. It is intriguing that he chose not to go to the pig pen where his son was suffering and did not attempt to make him feel at ease there. Instead, he patiently waited at home and kept a lookout for his prodigal son's return. Furthermore, he prepared for his homecoming. This approach demonstrates the father's foresight and wisdom. It also demonstrates faith in believing for what is unseen.

3. The scripture grants amazing insight regarding the father's choice regarding his son. It says, "when no one did anything for him, he (the prodigal) came to his senses." Going to the pig pen and making a prodigal comfortable can prevent him or her from coming to their own senses, and eventually returning home to their family and faith.

4. When the prodigal came to himself, he said, "I will arise and go to my father and say, I have sinned against God and my father." That's one key in recognizing a prodigal is ready to come home. A realization and understanding of what they have done, personal choices and actions of sin, admitting their sin, repenting of their sin, indicates a sincere readiness to come home to God is sustainable.

5. The son returns home and the father has already prepared a party for his return. Faith in action. Belief in promises God has spoken. Actively pursuing the answers of prayer.

And demonstrating an attitude of grace toward others and oneself. This is how miracles begin in the lives of people.

6. It's interesting that when the older son appears in the story, he is unhappy about the prodigal receiving such a welcome. But the father assures him by saying, "Everything I have is yours." The prodigal had squandered his inheritance and was not going to receive anything further from his father's estate. He would rightfully receive what is his. An attitude of acceptance and grace and forgiveness is vital to obtaining God's blessing and promises. Forgiving others and oneself. The latter, often being the most difficult thing to do in our lives.

Our family has lived this parable for four decades. Our daughter, unfortunately, continues to struggle and has yet to come to her senses. After sowing the seeds of rebellion for 40 years, the crop she has produced is challenging to deal with. We are fighting a constant battle for her soul, but despite everything, we continue to love and pray for her. The consequences of her choices have been severe, and her four children have experienced a great deal of pain as a result of her lifestyle.

Life's Challenges Are More Than Moments

I have found that life offers more mystery than answers at times. Faith is often lived out by accepting this strange paradox and trusting God through the confusion and mystery and struggle. The Bible's pages are filled with such dilemmas. Every book in Scripture has crisis moments where God's people, including the great men and women of faith, had more questions than answers. It was no different for me and my husband in the battle with our daughter.

In 2006, our daughter informed us that she and her four children were relocating from the Seattle area in Washington to Idaho for a job opportunity. Her two older boys, aged 14 and 16, were going to assist her with the move, and she required help with her younger children, a 10-year-old boy, and a 9-year-old girl. My husband suggested sending the younger children to stay with us while they moved, and we would fly them back once they were settled. Additionally, we decided to take them to Disneyland as a treat.

A few weeks before this, our church had taken a group on a pilgrimage to the Holy Land, where we visited several historical sites, including the Church of All Nations situated near the Garden of Gethsemane. One of the memorable places we visited was the altar made of a large rock outcropping, which is believed to be where Jesus prayed on the night he was betrayed. As I visited that site, I allowed my mind to go back in time and reimagine the scene in the Garden the night Jesus was betrayed. Tensions were high. Emotions on edge. Jesus and his disciples seemed to be on opposite ends of the spectrum emotionally, mentally, spiritually.

It appears Jesus knew what was going to take place. He understood this was part of the "Greater Plan." But in his humanness, he appears to be open to an alternative. Who really wants to die? To be tortured the way He was going to be tortured? Thus, he prayed, "Not my will but thine be done."

As I recalled that scene sitting in the place of its occurrence in Jerusalem, I felt God speak to me and ask, "Kaye, are you willing to pray that prayer? Are you willing to pray that prayer now?" Yes, Lord. Not my will but your will. Easier said than done as life was about to reveal that present challenges are often more than moments in time. They can be battles that rage on for years. For a lifetime.

CHAPTER 8

AFTER TWO WEEKS, our two youngest grandchildren arrived. We didn't know them well because our daughter was estranged from us. Despite that, we had a great time with them and took them to Disneyland. We had a wonderful 14-day trip.

When we returned home, we tried calling our daughter but couldn't reach her for three days. On the fourth day, we received a shocking call from Child Protective Services in Idaho, informing us that our daughter was in jail, and her two older boys had been placed in foster care.

We were in shock and unsure about what to do. The father of the two little ones lived in Washington, so we contacted and informed him what we had just learned about our daughter's situation and let him know we had his children in our care. We offered to send the children to him. His answer was swift and a definite no. "You keep them," he said. "They are better off with you than me."

After that phone call, I sat down and recalled the prayer I made at the Church of All Nations, "Not my will, but thine be done." I finally understood the question that God asked me during my prayer at the altar in Jerusalem. He had a task for me to fulfill, and I had already declared my willingness to do it.

Although the children were in shock when we received custody of them, we had already bonded during our trip to Disneyland. They felt secure and protected with us. My husband and I were 72, and 66 years of age respectively, and we suddenly found ourselves raising grade school children. We attended back-to-school nights, bought them school uniforms, and reorganized our home to accommodate them. Despite the challenges, we were grateful for the opportunity to care for our grandchildren and fulfill God's plan for our lives.

The children's physical, mental, and emotional condition was concerning. Their teeth were in poor shape, so I took them to a dentist who specialized in treating children. After the x-rays were taken, the estimated cost for their dental work was $3,000. I asked the dentist if she accepted Medi-Cal, which I had secured for the children. Unfortunately, the dentist said she did not take Medi-Cal patients. At that point, I requested the X-rays and prepared to leave. When the dentist returned with the x-rays, she surprised me by saying, "I am going to do their dental work this time pro-bono and I will apply for Medi-Cal so you can continue to bring the children to me for their dental care." God had provided a solution to my prayers, and I felt immense gratitude for the dentist's generosity.

Praying, "Not my will but thine be done," was a wonderful decision. It was clear that God's provision was available when I was living within His will and remained open to His leading and plans for my life. Provision is something God desires to do in our lives. He wants to meet our needs and provide answers to our challenges. This reality is a tremendous blessing and gift we sometimes lose sight of in our daily journey.

We enrolled the children in our church's elementary school when they were in the 4th and 5th grades. During this time, we discovered that our grandson in the 5th grade was unable to read. My husband felt led to devote his time to tutoring him for the entire school year, and our grandson was able to read by the end of the year. Our commitment to our two youngest grandchildren lasted for six years. Eventually, they returned to Idaho and reunited with their mother, where they lived for another six years.

God's Promptings Do Come Through Normal Channels

During the Christmas season, six years after our youngest grandchildren had left our home, our church organized an outreach for the community at large, called the "Bike and Toy Giveaway." It was aimed at helping underprivileged children identified by District School authorities. These children were invited to the event and presented with bicycles, clothing, and other necessary items needed for their care.

At the giveaway, a friend of ours who was aware of our situation sat down with us for a cup of coffee and inquired about our youngest grandson, who was now 22 years old. Regrettably, we were saddened to report we had no knowledge of his situation since we never heard from him.

On our way home from the event, I suggested to my husband that our friend's comment was a message from the Lord, and we should reach out and track our grandson down to check on him and see how he was doing. That evening we made the call and discovered that our grandson, at 22 years of age, was homeless. He was homeless and his life was in shambles. He was in desperate need of help. We asked if he would like to come and live with us again and he was so ready and willing.

Three years later, he still resides with us, and his life is being gradually restored to wholeness. We see once again how God spoke to us through our friend, leading to our grandson's return to our home. And today our grandson works at a car dealership owned by that very friend.

God uses normal and ordinary channels of life to prompt and inspire and guide and answer. Often, we miss what God is saying to our lives because we look for something extraordinary. We subconsciously think all answers and guidance are found in a "spiritual" setting and dismiss that God can use routine, daily life, a conversation with a friend to speak to us. God can speak anywhere and at any time. In a church, prayer, worship, Bible study, such "spiritual" places; and also, in everyday life occurrences. God can speak through a song in your car. He can speak as you're walking down the street. He can speak through something we encounter or see in the course of a day. He speaks through nature and events and with a still small voice. Are we listening?

Jesus said, "My sheep know my voice and they follow me." Hearing, listening, then, obediently following Jesus will never push you down the wrong path. Rather, it will take you on a journey filled with serendipitous moments, unthinkable situations, and unfathomable experiences. It all leads to a life of fulfillment, joy, and contentment. It won't always be easy and there will be difficulties and challenges and a million questions along the way. Yet, living God's way ultimately proves to be worthwhile, and grants a dimension of life and blessing unfound in the commonality of living.

What Did He Say?

A remarkable verse of scripture is found in the Book of John. If this was the only revelation God granted humanity, the only time

God ever spoke, it would be enough. This one verse found in the tenth chapter of the Book of John provides insight as to what God's plans are for one's life, and what the enemy's plans are for that same life. The verse is John 10:10. It reads like this:

> *"The thief's purpose is to steal and kill and destroy.*
> *My purpose is to give them a rich and satisfying life."*
> John 10:10 NLT

Other translations use the term, "I have come to give them an abundant life." Do you read what God says about your life? He came to give you a "rich and satisfying life." "An abundant life." Whereas the enemy comes to steal, to kill, to destroy. Do you see the progression in those terms? To steal means, "to take without right." God has dreams and plans for your life and the enemy comes in to steal what does not belong to him. He steals people's dreams, hopes. He steals the blessings God has prepared in advance for our lives. This is what happened in the life of our daughter. God had rich and satisfying plans for her. Because she refused to listen to God, to Godly counsel, she opened the floodgates, and the enemy came storming in to steal everything God had planned for her.

After the enemy steals, he takes the next step to kill. In the context of the passage, the word kill means, "to leave dead on the inside." Once the enemy steals dreams and hopes and blessings, one feels defeated inside. They feel dead, as if there is no purpose, so they slide deeper into sin because there is no power in their own strength to get out. And that leads to the enemy's ultimate goal which is to destroy. Destroy means, "to leave in complete ruins." Look around and see all the destruction in our world today. Some people's lives are in ruins and if you look deep, you'll find the pattern of steal-kill-destroy. Other lives are filled with goodness and blessing, and if you examine those lives, you'll notice the enemy's pattern of destruction is nonexistent. Oh, there certainly were instances of the enemy's methods and attacks on their lives. No one is immune. But that individual listened, fought, and resisted, believed God's promise for abundance, and thereby overcame the enemy's intentions of harm.

If you're in a place today where you are not experiencing abundance, your story is not over. Though the journey may be dark at this moment in your life, God desires to shower you with blessing and goodness. Hear. Listen. Obey. Reclaim what God has for you. Jesus said, "I have come to give you life, and life abundantly." Life that's more than survival. More than mediocrity. An abundant life that leads to fulfillment and unimagined blessing. Raise your head above the darkness that encases you. Look up. See the infinity of goodness that awaits. The abundant life God has promised you.

CHAPTER 9

IN 2016, THE church where my Husband and I served on staff commenced an annual fast. Our congregation initiated this strategic event by coming together at "the wall" to seek God. That evening began a new journey in my walk with God. Something deep and profound. I'm going to share this journey with you. And the reason I want to share this story is because of the unique way that God chooses to direct us.

"The Wall" is a monthly prayer service held at our church. Hundreds attend this gathering, and we experience incredible moments of God's outpouring. There is something powerful about Christians gathering corporately to pray. To pray for our nation, city, leaders. To pray for others, and the needs of others. To pray for distant lands and the body of Christ throughout the world. To pray for healing: mental, emotional, physical, and spiritual. To pray for our families and our own needs. And to pray for guidance and direction for our personal lives.

Throughout my adult life, I have relied on discovering truth from God's Word and applying His principles as my guide. However, this time, God's direction unfolded not only in principle but also through specific steps as He spoke to me through His Word. It was one little word that God used to take me on this journey.

At the start of our fast, my husband and I were in the midst of yet another crisis with our daughter. Unfortunately, this is a recurring pattern in our relationship with her. She tends to create chaos and gravitates towards people who are also prone to crises. Throughout her adult life, we have experienced periods of extended silence from her, sometimes lasting months or even years. About a year had passed since we had last heard from her until just before Christmas when we received alarming news. Our daughter's life was in danger due to a relationship she had with a man she had met at an AA meeting. They had lived together for six months, and when she decided not to marry him, he became angry and threatened her life. The breakup caused him to relapse into drug addiction, and he began stalking her. Fear drove her to move out of state to find safety, and we had no idea any of this was happening at the time.

In his drug-induced state of anger over the breakup, the man went searching for our daughter and found her. Early one morning, he broke into her home and held her at gunpoint, threatening to kill her. Fortunately, a friend who was there was able to break free, grab a gun, and after pleading with the intruder to stop beating our daughter, he was forced to kill the ex-boyfriend in self-defense. Our daughter called us at that point to tell us what happened, but the communication was brief, and we didn't hear from her again for a few weeks.

This was the crisis my husband and I were facing as our church embarked on that fast in January of 2016. We always include our daughter and her children on our prayer list each year during the fast, and this year was no exception. On the first day of the fast at "The Wall," our pastor asked us all to enter into a time of quiet prayer. He encouraged us to pray the prayer, "Speak Lord, for your servant is listening." And so, I did.

What Did He Say?

And He answered. Just one word: GO! In some sense, that little word is commonplace in the church world, used frequently and often, referring mostly to reaching others with the gospel. As Jesus said, "GO into all the world and preach the gospel." Thus, we hear the word "GO" frequently in church services. We also encounter it frequently when we read the Bible. It's easy to think this little word is for missionaries and evangelists, those engaged in full-time ministry on a global scale. We dismiss it as a word instructing the church corporately to engage the ultimate mission of the kingdom of God, to spread the gospel to the ends of the earth. Due to the commonality, it's easy to overlook that God may use this little word to speak into our personal lives.

When God spoke that word into my heart at "The Wall," I knew it was no coincidence. In my personal devotions, I had recently read the book of Jonah and was struck by the interesting provisions that God provided for Jonah. When God first spoke to Jonah and told him to "go to Nineveh," Jonah ran away. However, even during his disobedience and after he finally obeyed, the scriptures say that God provided several things for him - a storm, a great fish, a shrub, a worm, and an east wind.

These provisions from God do not fit into our typical understanding of what provision looks like. When we think of provision, we often think of things like financial provision, great relationships, opportunities for ministry, and God meeting our specific needs the way we think they should or will be met. However, God's provision for Jonah shows us that God's ways are higher than our ways, and He may provide for us in unexpected and unconventional ways.

In Jonah's case, God's provision of the storm and the great fish was used to get Jonah's attention and bring him back to the task

God had given him. The shrub was a temporary comfort for Jonah, but it was also a way for God to teach him a lesson about the value of things that are fleeting. The worm and the east wind were used to bring about the destruction of the shrub and to further teach Jonah about the sovereignty of God.

So, while financial provision, great relationships, opportunities for ministry, and expected or hoped-for responses are certainly good things, we should also recognize that God's provision and answers may come in unexpected ways and for unexpected purposes. It is our job to trust in Him and His plan, even when it doesn't align with our own understanding or desires.

As I considered the concept of God's provision and His call for me to "Go," God spoke to me again. This time, He assured me that His provision would prepare me for the destination that He had determined for me. He urged me to pay attention to what He considered provision, even if it did not fit into my own understanding or expectations. Through these circumstances, He was preparing the way for me to go to an unknown destination.

One morning during the Church fast, I came across another scripture where God said "Go" to someone. This time, it was Abraham, whom God told to "Go to the land I will show you." I began to see a pattern that every time God said "Go" in the scripture, it was a call to action. It was direction from God and God was using this word to give me direction. I now had three different instructions from God:

1. I was to **"Go."**
2. God was providing circumstances to prepare the way for me to **"Go."**
3. And now I was in a process where He would show me where to **"Go."**

With these three instructions from God, I was beginning to understand that I needed to trust in Him and follow His lead, even if it meant stepping into the unknown. So, I resolved to heed God's call to "Go," trust in His provision, and await His guidance for the destination that He had prepared for me.

Confirmation From God

When God speaks to our hearts, He often provides confirmation from various sources. Though we live in a visible world, our faith operates in the invisible world, things we hope for but cannot see in the visible realm. Faith is a profound struggle that encompasses our unwavering trust in God's power, while also grappling with our own insecurities and fleeting uncertainties regarding whether God can utilize us or communicate directly with us. Therefore, God does confirm what he's calling us to do.

In my case, God used the Bible and an individual to confirm what He was speaking to my heart. I came across another scripture that provided further guidance for me. This time, it was Luke 15:4, which said, "Go after the one which is lost. Leave the 99 and go." Reading this passage, I realized where I needed to go—to my lost child. I pleaded with God, knowing that only He could make this happen for me to reach my daughter.

The following Sunday, our pastor delivered a sermon on 1 Samuel 16:1-2. This passage recounted the story of God sending the prophet Samuel to anoint a king. The scripture said, "Go... I am sending you, for I have provided for myself a King!" At that moment, God granted me understanding of why I was being called to go.

These scriptures, Luke 15:4 and 1 Samuel 16:1-2, revealed to me the path I needed to take. I was to leave behind the familiar and comfortable (represented by the 99 sheep and the existing king) and pursue my lost child, just as Samuel was sent to anoint a new king. God was directing me to go and bring my daughter back, for He had a purpose and a plan for her life.

The Goodness of God

What Did He Say?

1. I had clarity on where I was to GO.
2. I recognized that God was providing everything I needed for the journey.
3. I understood how I was to proceed.
4. Most importantly, I grasped that God desired something for Himself.

Following this realization, I received more direction from another message spoken by our pastor. His points from the story of the blind man in John 9 resonated with me. Three aspects of this powerful story of healing spoke to my heart. First, Jesus affirmed that neither the blind man nor his parents sinned. Nothing anyone did in life's decisions caused the man's blindness. It was a consequence of life and life rains on the just and unjust. This realization granted me great freedom. The situation with my daughter was not my fault, nor the fault of our family. Secondly, the purpose of the man's blindness was for the works of God to be displayed in him. When our daughter returns to the fold, it will be for God's glory. Finally, the man remained blind in God's presence until he obeyed Jesus' instructions. Only then was he healed. Jesus commanded him, "Go, wash in the pool of Siloam." The man embraced those instructions. He entered the pool, washed, and returned home with restored sight.

As I pondered this story, I realized the command to "Go" was for our daughter. Yet, I could only be obedient to the call, and I could not personally change anything or anyone. She had to be obedient to what God was saying to her. It would be up to her to obey God to receive her healing.

Listening to God's voice, even if He speaks just a single two-letter word, holds immense significance. Throughout this journey, I have discovered the importance of dedicating time to listen and paying close attention while reading God's Word for His divine guidance. Every direction I have shared has been discovered during my encounters with God's Word. I earnestly asked Him to communicate with me, and He responded. His message was conveyed through the pastor's sermons, the scriptures in Jonah and 1 Samuel, and my diligent study of His Word.

God leads us step by step, unfolding His plan gradually. This difficult story commenced in December of 2015, and three months later, we embarked on a journey to visit our daughter. It was through God's Word that we were equipped to confront this challenging situation. Although the story is not yet complete, we are currently in the process of receiving our miracle because God has made a promise, saying, "Now, do not be afraid; continue to believe, and she will be restored!

CHAPTER 10

"And the Lord will continually guide you and satisfy your desire in scorched places and give strength to your bones; and you will be like a watered garden, and like a spring of water whose waters do not fail. And those from among you will rebuild the ancient ruins you will raise up the age-old foundations; and you will be called the repairer of the breach, the restorer of the streets in which to dwell." Isaiah 58:11 & 12

IN JULY, 1986, the weather in Concord, California was hot. The hills were dry, and the heat was stifling. My husband, Harley, and I had traveled from the State of Washington to meet with the Pastoral Search Committee at Calvary Temple Church. The committee's task was to find a new pastor to lead a rather small congregation of approximately 250 people.

Back in the Seventies, during Harley's time as a businessman at an office furniture company in San Francisco, we had attended this very church. We served as lay people, teaching a Sunday School class for young married couples. Now, a decade later, those couples we once taught had risen to positions on the Church Board. It was delightful to reconnect with these board members, but our visit held a serious purpose. These individuals were now part of the Pastoral Search Committee responsible for hiring a new pastor. Meanwhile, Harley and I, had transitioned out of the business world and devoted ourselves to full-time ministry in Spokane, Washington.

We spent several days engaging with the committee in various settings, and on this particular day, Harley went to meet with them while I remained in our rather dim and dreary hotel room. Admittedly, the accommodations were far from ideal, a fact my husband often jokingly highlighted by claiming the motel was so bad that they stole our personal towels. In truth, the church's financial difficulties necessitated these modest lodgings. The church desperately needed a new pastor, which is why we found ourselves enduring the July heatwave in Concord.

As Harley left for the meeting, I felt compelled to spend some time in prayer, knowing that the committee would soon ask us for a decision. Would we accept the position of Lead Pastor at Calvary Temple Church in Concord? Although I understood that ultimately it was Harley's decision, I yearned to receive guidance from God myself. Clutching my Bible, I resumed reading from where I had left off the day before in the book of Isaiah. Before delving into the scriptures, I paused to pray and beseeched God to personally guide me.

We were content in our pastoral role in Spokane, Washington, and God had been showering blessings upon both the church and the work we were involved in. It was difficult to comprehend why God would want us to abandon a thriving congregation for a financially troubled one. How could such a circumstance align with His plan for our lives?

What Did He Say?

As I read the scripture that day, God spoke clearly through his word in Isaiah 58:11-12. The passage reads:

> *"And the Lord will continually guide you and <u>satisfy your desire in scorched places</u> and give strength to your bones; and you will be like a watered garden, and like a spring of water whose waters do not fail. And those from among you will rebuild the ancient ruins. You will raise up the age-old foundations; and you will be called the repairer of the breach, the restorer of the streets in which to dwell."*

It's stunning how God's word is alive and able to speak to our given challenges and circumstances at any given moment in our lives. God is always ready and willing to guide us when we take the time to listen. His Spirit will guide us into all truth. On that morning that is what I needed. I wanted an answer to my questions, clear guidance from Him. I was seeking confirmation for our future and found it in His word. And this is exactly what God provided. As I read, **"satisfy your desire in scorched places,"** I knew God was calling us to leave the Northwest and accept the pastorate in Concord. He would satisfy our desire in a scorched place. Not in the beautiful northwest, but in a scorched place.

How often can we reasonably expect our desires in life to be fulfilled in a scorched place? Or a desolate and barren place? I had never considered the possibility of finding satisfaction there.

However, as I continued reading through that passage of scripture, God proclaimed, "You will be like a well-watered garden and a never-failing spring of water."

As I read, I became increasingly excited to share these truths with Harley. The Spirit of God was guiding and leading. I continued to read and came across a remarkable promise in verse 12: "Those among you will rebuild the ancient ruins; you will raise up the age-old foundations and be called the repairer of the breach, the restorer of the streets to dwell in."

What did God just say? The guidance I received that afternoon was specifically directed toward us. The words "You will" became crystal clear. It was us. We were being called to assume this position. Regardless of how hopeless and dire the situation seemed, God had exciting plans for our future and for the church.

As Christians, there are moments in our lives where we can receive specific instruction and confirmation from God. He desires to lead and guide us through every situation and dilemma we face. Good or bad. But we must seek Him, we must spend time in His word and LISTEN. When the answers arrive, when He speaks to our hearts, there is an otherworldly feeling that rushes through our spirits. As if something burst inside, filling us with chills and goosebumps and over-the-top confidence. Suddenly, we see what we couldn't see. Obstacles that appeared oppressive diminish. Massive mountains that stood in the way shrink into rolling hills. Our entire perspective changes and faith that once hoped now believes.

Now I understood that God was summoning us to this desolate place. It was precisely where He wanted us to serve Him. I realized that the scorched place would be transformed into a lush garden, a spring of living water that would never run dry. The prospect of others rising up to help us rebuild was an incredible source of encouragement.

Obedience, Faith, and God's Humor

Once God speaks, we must step out in obedience and trust. Faith in action. If we were going to experience God's promises, we had to leave the lush place of blessing, of success, for the scorched place of struggle and failure. And so, we did. On September 1, 1986, we assumed responsibilities at Calvary Temple.

God has a wonderful sense of humor. Scripture is filled with stories and encounters and tales where one must laugh. The Bible proves the human journey is truly a comedy of errors. God allows humorous moments in our lives to remind: As we take the trip of life, enjoy the whole journey. The entire journey. All aspects of the journey. The good and bad. And those moments filled with irony and hilarity.

I mentioned earlier, Harley had left the business world and entered the ministry in December, 1979. Prior to this transition, His career was in sales of high-end office furniture in the Bay Area. So as Harley walked into the office assigned to the Lead Pastor on his first day in Concord, he was greeted by a desk with three legs, supported by bricks in place of the missing fourth leg. The irony struck him deeply. He had gone from the penthouse to the outhouse, so to speak, as he settled into his new office. A man who sold the best office furniture in the world now sat behind a broken desk. God's humor on full display. Laughter amidst carnage.

That incident marked the beginning of many surprises and challenges that were unknown when we accepted the position at Calvary Temple. Moments of discovery revealed the desperate state of the church's finances, the negative reputation it had in the community due to unpaid bills, and the looming threat of foreclosure on adjacent properties that were purchased for expansion. We discovered just how scorched this place was in all types of dimensions.

The most heart-wrenching revelation was that the missions' budget amounted to a mere $6,000 per year, and that missionaries had not received any support for the previous six months. This news brought Harley to tears. In the early stages of our recovery, we ensured that the committed funds reached the missionaries as we struggled to pay the church's bills and debts.

Despite the difficulties, God remained faithful, and gradually people began returning to the church. As word spread about the newfound accountability and integrity in financial matters, monetary contributions started flowing. Additionally, individuals with musical talents joined us, offering their gifts and talents to serve God. While we couldn't afford to hire staff, many volunteers readily stepped up to serve in various capacities. It was our own community that helped us rebuild the age-old foundations. Our hearts and minds filled with excitement, and God blessed our ministry. Things that followed were both challenging and astounding. And contagious.

CHAPTER 11

WHAT DID THE once scorched place of Concord, California look like as it blossomed into a well-watered garden? Contagious with possibility. The first sign of life was our ability to pay the church bills and clear the properties of debt, effectively averting foreclosure. Secondly, God graciously provided the necessary funds for us to hire new staff. Our first hire was a brilliant youth pastor, followed by a young couple who joined as Young Marrieds pastors, having previously worked with us in Spokane. Another gifted couple took on the role of music pastors, and eventually, our son and his wife joined the staff as youth pastors. The church experienced both financial and numerical growth, with people discovering Christ and actively serving Him within the church. It truly became a fruitful and thriving community. A place of contagious faith and joy and hope.

As the church grew, bursting at the seams, we needed to expand. The realization of needing a new building became evident. Our current location was landlocked and would not allow for expansion to meet the size of the congregation. It became obvious we wouldn't be a neighborhood church; we would become a regional church.

We needed a new location, new land. No easy task in Contra Costa County, one of the most expensive and built-out counties in the world.

We embarked on a search for a property spanning 7 to 10 acres in and around the Concord area, a pursuit that spanned three years. Over the course of those years, one realtor threw in the towel, informing my husband, "Don't call me anymore. You lack the funds and won't stumble upon a suitable piece of property." In true Harley fashion, my husband retorted, "It's a shame, given the substantial commission you will be forfeiting."

After some time, we received a surprise call from a realtor one afternoon: "I found a piece of property that I think you ought to look at. It's on a freeway and is visible from the freeway. I think this will meet your needs," the voice on the other end said.

Upon laying my eyes on the property, an immediate realization washed over me – this was the property we had tirelessly sought. Despite the presence of significant gas lines traversing the land and a network of power lines above, steep hills on both ends, this property was visible from the freeway and seen by thousands of commuters every single day. The 38 acres were perfect to suit our needs. But the property was not for sale and the owners were located on the East Coast. Another blessing in disguise.

The challenges of the property, gas and power lines, steep terrain, made only half of the 38 acres suitable for development. Obstacles that deterred developers and others seeking land were used by God to grant favor to us. In an effort to seize the opportunity, we penned a letter to the proprietor, extending an offer of $750,000. Let me remind you, this encompassed 38 acres adjacent to a freeway, offering optimal visibility, in one of the most expensive counties in the world. Much to our elation, the offer was accepted, albeit contingent on one stipulation – we were to cover the real estate fee on top of the offering price. Eagerly, we consented.

Collaborating with our architect, we developed a campus layout that eventually birthed what we now know as THE BAY CHURCH in Concord, CA. The gas lines and power lines were suitable for our parking requirements. The steep hills on the ends of the property worked well to protect our property from interference with neighboring properties. And today if you visit the church, you see adequate parking, great ingress, and egress. Traveling along Highway 4 through Concord, one's gaze invariably alights upon a beautiful church building where thousands of people worship every week.

A Sense of Inadequacy

After serving in Concord for several years, Harley approached me with an intriguing proposition. He expressed concern about our limited outreach to the singles population in Contra Costa County, which comprised 40% of the total demographic. In light of this, he asked if I would consider leading a singles ministry at Calvary Temple.

I was taken aback. Being single has never been a personal experience for me, as I transitioned directly from my parents' home to marriage. I possessed no knowledge or understanding of the single lifestyle, nor have I ever ministered to men. All my previous experience in ministry had been to women. After recovering from the shock of Harley's suggestion, I was curious as to why he asked me, so I inquired. I asked my husband, "How did you come up with my name to lead the singles ministry?" He responded, "Pray about it." What? No clarification. No explanation. Just, "pray about it."

The reason I was seeking more from my husband was because of my own sense of inadequacy. Often, God calls us to tasks and events where we feel unqualified and inadequate. And the enemy uses that sense of insufficiency to rob our lives of tremendous blessing. Ironically, my husband reminded me of what I knew I needed to do. A three-legged desk on bricks all over again. Now it was my turn to sit behind that desk.

I couldn't help but feel inadequate, knowing my lack of expertise in the realm of singleness and what singles face in their lives. And singleness stretches wide and far: Young singles. Divorced singles. Single parents. Singles in a relationship. Singles that remain single. A kaleidoscope of singleness and what could I possibly say to this demographic when I never experienced it myself? Despite my reservations, I earnestly prayed, recognizing that God alone understands the extent of my limitations. And He understands singleness.

What Did He Say?

"Call to me and I will answer you and show you great and mighty things which you do not know."
Jeremiah 33:3

Oh, my goodness! There it was the answer I had been seeking. Though I knew I needed to reach out to God on this matter, I was blinded for a moment by my inadequacy. Though I knew I needed to turn to the Word for guidance, I focused on circumstance. Human frailty on full display. Something we all encounter in our lives. Even the greats in the Bible who experienced monumental answers to prayer, who witnessed God perform acts of impossibility, experienced similar feelings, and spiritual setbacks. Times of forgetfulness of who God is and what He can do. Abraham. Noah. David. Elijah. Paul. Peter. The list is endless.

In my doubt, and sense of inadequacy, I returned to His Word. The Scriptures reminded me: If I call upon God, He will respond and reveal. He could teach me extraordinary and unknown things about singles. Excitedly, I shared this scripture with Harley, expressing my willingness to shoulder the responsibility.

The next challenge was finding a suitable space within the church for our meetings. Our church was in the midst of a building program, and it would take approximately a year for the construction to be completed. Our current location could not facilitate meetings for this large demographic. Undeterred, Harley embarked on a research quest and stumbled upon a space in a shopping mall near our church. We promptly secured the facility and commenced our ministry dedicated to serving singles.

Now that we had a facility, I still had no idea about how I should minister to singles. So again, I sought His guidance. I felt directed to observe the singles who attended our church. I believed God said, "Look at the singles you currently have in the church. Make sure they're attractive, well-spoken, friendly, and love God. This group is to be your leadership team."

Attraction. That was puzzling. Beauty is in the eye of the beholder. I didn't believe God's instruction simply meant physical attraction. But spiritually attractive. To seek out individuals who displayed energy, excitement, who conveyed a radiant love for God. These individuals were to form our core leadership team. Acting on God's instructions, I carefully selected singles who exhibited natural leadership qualities and displayed those aforementioned attributes of attractiveness. Once the team was selected, we launched.

As the ministry commenced, and grew, it became apparent that we should expand our efforts to reach all singles in our community.

While we had established a solid leadership foundation within our group, I recognized the necessity of equipping them with the skills to lead singles in outreach endeavors. And this led to an exciting adventure of reaching singles from all walks of life in our community. God led us to think outside the box.

CHAPTER 12

WHEN GOD SPEAKS to our lives, we can expect the unexpected. The Bible is filled with stories that defy comprehension. And most of these narratives involve individuals, real flesh and blood individuals like you and me. . . ordinary people.

Most miracles begin with an idea. God inspires someone with a thought that leads to action. Build an Ark. Walk around a city seven times. Dip in the river five times. Challenge the giant. On and on it goes throughout the Old Testament. Strange stories with incredible outcomes and results. The New Testament follows with more detailed events of God speaking to individuals, who then obeyed, and witnessed astonishing and life-changing and life-giving results.

God desires to involve us in His work because He knows that's where we find true fulfillment. To live in such a realm requires we hear and listen to His voice. That we engage His leadings and promptings in our lives. To not only hear but believe what He is speaking to our hearts. And sometimes that means to think outside the box, to see what we cannot see.

Once we had secured the leadership team of the Singles Ministry, we met together and sought the heart of God as a group. We prayed for insight and direction, specifically how we could reach the single population in our community.

What Did He Say?

During our leadership group prayer times, we gained insight and direction. God's direction opened doors into unchartered waters of knowledge and guidance on how we should proceed. It became clear that we should start by reaching out to the children of single parents. Now my own uncertainties extended not only to the realm of guiding singles but also to the complexities of ministering to children. I didn't have any idea how to minister to children, so I met with our children's pastor and she became excited about the idea of reaching out to the children of single parents in our community.

She suggested that we create a special event and call it "FRIDAY NIGHT LIVE." A vision unfolded to transform the church sanctuary into a carnival for children. A delightful evening was meticulously planned, where parents could forge new connections while their children enjoyed a secure and enjoyable environment of entertainment and fun.

The idea of a carnival caught on and the existing single community within the church embraced the event and volunteered to be the workers at the carnival and the event for single parents. As a result, our ministry expanded to encompass more than 200 singles who congregated for Sunday morning classes, accompanied by a considerable influx of children attending our church. In this process, God was showing us great and mighty things. I gained remarkable insights on how to reach and minister to people outside my knowledge and comfort zone.

As the group continued to flourish, it spanned a wide age range, encompassing singles aged 19 to 70. Recognizing the need for adaptation during this phase, I proposed a restructuring to our leadership team. This led to the subdivision of our singles ministry into three distinct groups, each with dedicated leadership. These groups initiated age-appropriate social activities. This idea came from God because it provided so many singles leadership positions in ministry. A captivating facet of this transformation was that singles collaborated closely in ministry, fostering connections as they contributed across various aspects. Through this, many beautiful marriages blossomed, cemented not only by time but also by their shared dedication to serving God within their respective churches.

Another initiative we developed took place on Thursday evenings and was named "Thursday Night at the Movies." Our facility was configured with three separate "theatres," featuring teachings on subjects such as single parenting, financial management, and spiritual growth. The topics were periodically rotated, providing valuable insights to singles. Simultaneously, Christian movies catered to the children of singles, creating an event both groups anticipated eagerly. These gatherings consistently featured a coffee shop setup, generously donated by a member of our church to support our singles ministry. This not only facilitated fundraising but also added to the overall benefit of the ministry.

I'm deeply grateful to God for unveiling many wonderful ways to engage with singles, methods initially beyond my own understanding. The process simply required reaching out to God and attentively listening to His guidance. True to His promise of revealing "great and mighty things which I did not know," He remained faithful. He provided everything needed to engage a task I was not intellectually or educationally prepared to do. As a result, we successfully reached a significant portion of the single population in our Contra Costa County.

Gardens In the Desert

Harley and I dedicated 15 years of our lives to serving God at Calvary Temple (The Bay Church) in Concord, California, before transitioning into retirement from full-time ministry. During our time there, the church flourished, and we impacted thousands of lives throughout the region. We witnessed the profound transformation of so many who found the Lord in our services. Both in and outside the church building.

Our efforts led to the establishment of an annual outdoor event celebrated in the region called "The Singing Flag." This spectacle ministered to tens of thousands as we honored the heritage of our Christian nation. Our efforts led to the formation of an exceptional staff, and as we concluded our tenure, we were gratified to see the church's remarkable financial standing. Notably, the missions' budget for our last year at Calvary Temple was $500,000.

God was faithful to His word. Calvary Temple indeed became a well-watered garden in the desert. The scorched land to which we arrived fifteen years earlier was lush with life and growth and unlimited possibility. With unwavering commitment, God remained true to His promises. Calvary Temple blossomed into a metaphorical oasis, symbolizing the spiritual abundance that was cultivated. Our aspirations for ministry were fulfilled in ways that exceeded our imagination. The community that grew around us played a pivotal role in revitalizing the timeless principles that restored the foundations of faith. In this regard, we were bestowed with the honor of being referred to as "repairers of the breach" and "restorers of the streets in which to dwell."

Looking back, my heart overflows with gratitude for God's Word. I'm so grateful that He speaks. Every single day He speaks into our lives. We must pause and listen. Slow down. Take time to hear what He is saying. It was through His guidance and communication that we were able to contribute to the incredible journey we had in Concord. Watching a desolate land morph into lush gardens of life.

What Is He Saying to You?

God deeply desires to involve you in all His plans and dreams for your life. He hopes to fulfill your desires. Never give up and do not give in. If you are in a desolate, scorched place today, there is a well-watered garden awaiting you. Call to Him and He will answer you. He will show you great and mighty things you do not know. Lend your ear and heart and mind to Him. Open up. What is He saying to you? Are you listening to His voice? Engage His Word. You will find answers and direction. Seek Him and find Him. He is waiting for you.

Created For Purpose

Every person has experienced moments of doubt, confusion, and failure. We've all experienced times when life turns our world upside down and we need answers that seem nowhere to be found. We stare at our surroundings and cannot envision how the scorched land of our present turmoil will ever become beautiful, will ever find growth and life and hope again. But that's an illusion the enemy uses in our lives to keep us from moving forward to discover God's plans and hopes for our lives.

From the beginning of time, God has desired to communicate with His creation. He has desired to involve us in His work. To give us purpose and a sense of mission in life. He instituted this idea when He created mankind. Adam, situated by God in the Garden, was granted a specific mission for his existence. God gave Adam purpose in the arena of life where he had placed him.

> *"Then the Lord God took the man and put him into the Garden of Eden to cultivate it and keep it . . . and out of the ground the Lord formed every beast of the field and every bird of the sky and brought them to the man to see what he would call them; and whatever the man called a living creature, that was its name."* Genesis 2:15 & 19 b

This is the pattern, the blueprint for life, that God has established with His creation. It's also a driving force behind His desire to engage in dialogue and companionship with us. He longs to entrust us with tasks, to foster a relationship so intimate that we can discern His voice as we navigate each day. Scripture recounts that Adam and Eve heard His footsteps in the Garden they called home. Can we perceive His presence where we are? Can you? Does His voice resonate through your challenges, your pain, in opportunities presented or withheld? Can you catch a glimpse of His promptings for your life in the counsel of others?

God has things He wants to say to us every day. He speaks constantly and consistently. Are we listening? A distinct purpose accompanies each of us, replete with actions tailored for the present day in our unique surroundings and environment. Adam's assignments harmonized with his immediate surroundings. God is not calling us to name creatures or tend to Eden's lush garden, for our placements differ. Just as Adam's tasks harmonized with his locale, God designs tasks for you, precisely where you reside. He has specific assignments for your life. What mission has He entrusted to you?

Occasionally, God appoints demanding tasks amidst arid land-scapes. Difficult assignments in scorched places. Yet, when we walk with Him, converse with Him, and heed His voice and follow His direction, He helps us find fulfillment and success. Even in barren lands, He transforms desolation into an oasis. A scorched place into a well-watered garden.

CHAPTER 13

I will stand at my guard post and station myself on
the ramparts. I will watch to see what He will say
to me, and how I should answer when corrected."
Habakkuk 2:1

IN THE MARGINS of my New American Standard
Bible are personal notes containing dates and short statements.
These notations are related to words that God has spoken to me
at important moments in my life. Such is the case with the above
verse from Habakkuk. God spoke that verse to me on August 20,
1980, at a very crucial moment when I needed direction.

My husband, Harley, and I had left the corporate world to ded-
icate ourselves to full-time ministry. Unfortunately, our timing was
less than ideal as the real estate market took a downturn, and our
waterfront home in Bellevue, Washington, didn't sell as planned.
This situation had significant consequences, requiring us to make
mortgage payments for both our Bellevue residence and a rental
property in Spokane, Washington, where we felt called to pastor.

The transition from the business world to ministry had greatly reduced our income, and over several months, our savings dwindled.

Harley and I had a candid conversation about our financial predicament, and he proposed a solution he believed would address our challenges. "Kaye, it's time for you to find employment," he suggested. Unfortunately for me, I had already found fulfillment in my ministry work, primarily conducting a daytime ladies' Bible study—a first for me and a role I cherished. It was my first opportunity to minister to women and I loved teaching God's Word. Harley's proposal to seek high-paying employment left me disheartened, as it clashed with my calling.

I understood the importance of submitting to Harley's leadership for the sake of our family, even though I strongly disagreed with his decision. As was my habit, I turned to the Bible and sought divine guidance through prayer. During my personal devotional Bible reading, I was immersed in the book of Genesis, where God spoke to me through the life of Abraham. I came across this passage:

> *"After these things the word of the Lord came to Abram in a vision saying, 'Do not fear, Abram, I am a shield to you; Your reward shall be very great."*
> Genesis 15:1

What Did He Say?

God gave me a promise when I was wrestling with feelings, and with something I did not want to do. I was in a great place spiritually, fulfilled and pursuing what I felt called to do. And then life's circumstances encroached. As they do to all of us.

God spoke to me, saying, "Do not fear, Kaye, I am a shield to you; Your reward shall be very great." I was elated by this message from God. In my mind, being a shield meant that God would protect me from needing employment. He would safeguard my position as a Bible Study teacher for the young women in our church. Not only would He shield me, but He would also reward me. I was filled with joy at this word from the Lord!

So, willingly submitting to Harley's advice, the next morning I got up and prepared to search for a job. I left our home with more confidence than I had ever felt while job hunting because I firmly believed in my heart that God would prevent me from finding employment. After all, He was my shield! Additionally, I was expecting a reward from God. I visited an employment agency, dressed up and brimming with confidence. They informed me of a job opening at a computer company.

I thought, "Perfect!" I had never laid hands on a computer before. Personal computers were not yet on the market, and businesses using automation connected to large offsite computers via telephone lines. Software wasn't readily available "off the shelf" back then; programmers custom-wrote software for businesses. I knew absolutely nothing about computers.

I met with the company's president, who explained the job: they needed someone to write documentation for custom-written software for end-users. He then led me to a computer and asked me to compose a letter explaining why they should hire me, using the computer, and print it out. With a few instructions from the president, I sat down to write the letter.

Surprisingly, I managed to write the letter and print it as he had instructed. I was told to return to his office once the task was completed. To my astonishment, he said, "You're hired!" On my way home, I cried. I couldn't help but cry out, "God, I thought you were going to protect me. I believed you were my shield. I thought I would receive a reward from you, allowing me to continue teaching my Bible Study." You had promised me a reward!"

God's ways are not our ways. I believed God was going to reward me in ways that were absolutely beyond my imagination. So, what was my reward, my "great" reward? God tends to enlarge our perception and idea of what we think we will obtain through obedience; what we think we deserve. The story of Joseph in the book of Genesis resonates this concept of how God's rewards and promises are so much larger than our own thoughts and plans. And so, it was for me when I chose to listen, trust, and press forward in obedience.

Promises Fulfilled in Unexpected Ways

In the same manner that the story of Joseph in Genesis 17 reveals that one's dreams and hopes can take strange twists and turns on a path of obedience leading to fulfillment, God did the same in my situation. A series of unexpected blessings surfaced in my life that brought fulfillment and granted numerous rewards.

First, shortly after I started working at the computer company, I was dispatched to one of our customer sites to provide training on computer software. That client happened to be The Federal Land Bank. I cultivated a relationship with the Supervisor of one of the Departments where I conducted training, and before long, I received a job offer from the bank that promised a much brighter future than what the computer company had in store for me. Indeed, there was a rewarding outcome.

Secondly, when I could no longer teach the morning Bible Study in Spokane to a small group of approximately 20 young mothers, our Pastor's wife presented me with a different ministry opportunity within our church. She entrusted me with the responsibility of overseeing an all-church event for the ladies, called Joy Fellowship, which was a monthly gathering. This allowed me to continue my ministry and remain obedient to what God had personally revealed to me through His Word. The reward lay in ministering to all the women in our church as opposed to a small group.

Third, during our time in Spokane, I had the privilege of automating the church office and the accounting department, which was another rewarding aspect of our ministry. As for what God had said to me, "Do not fear, Kaye ... Your reward shall be very great," it was truly gratifying to witness how God used these newfound opportunities and ministry roles. The reward God promised came in the form of personal fulfillment, and ministry expansion. They were rewards I could not foresee when God spoke the promise. The evening ministry leadership role, in particular, had a more significant impact than the small group of women who gathered to study the Bible with me.

About two years later, Harley and I received a call to join the staff at Capital Christian Center in Sacramento, CA. We were already familiar with Pastor Glen Cole's ministry, as Harley had encountered it during his years in the business world when we attended a church where Pastor Cole served as a staff pastor. We firmly believed that God was guiding us to leave Spokane and make the move to Sacramento.

Once again, I found myself needing to secure employment in our new community. It's intriguing that there happened to be a Federal Land Bank located just about a mile from Capital Christian Center. It was then that I recalled the promise from God spoken earlier. What did He say? "Your reward will be very great." It became evident that God was rewarding me for my obedience to His will and my husband's leadership in our family. Upon our arrival in

Sacramento, I was blessed with a wonderful job opportunity at the Federal Land Bank.

Drawing from my experiences in automation during the 1980s, I was able to apply that knowledge to automate our church offices when we served as Lead Pastors at Calvary Temple Church in Concord, CA. To this day, the benefits of those automation experiences continue to enrich our personal lives.

The rewards we've reaped have extended into various dimensions of our lives. One of the most valuable lessons I gleaned from this journey is that God's ways are not always our ways. And when He makes a promise, He unfailingly fulfills every promise He makes.

CHAPTER 14

"For My thoughts are not your thoughts, nor are your ways My ways," says the LORD. For as the heavens are higher than the earth, so are My ways higher than your ways, and My thoughts than your thoughts." Isaiah 55:8-9 NKJV

OBEDIENCE PRODUCES REWARDS in our lives. This concept is seen throughout Scripture. You find this lived out in every book of the Bible. Take a journey though the lives of a plethora of characters and find this pattern. Abraham on Mt. Moriah. Jacob and Esau. Joseph in Egypt. Moses in the desert. The spies entering Canaan. Joshua leading his people around Jericho. Rahab, the prostitute, protecting God's people. Elijah on Mt. Carmel. David and Goliath. On and on it goes throughout the Old Testament Stories of obedience launching miraculous victory and producing great rewards through obedience to what God says to each of our lives.

We see the same model throughout the New Testament as well, from Matthew through Acts, the pattern of obedience enlarged in even greater measure. Mind boggling stories of obedience birthing astonishing miracles that blessed multitudes and stunned sinners. It's no wonder the Christians in Acts were identified as those "who turned the world upside down." Radical obedience produces astounding results. Not just for the one who is obedient, but for all those connected to the individual who is obedient. The ripple effect.

God is all-knowing, and His understanding encompasses the entire span of our lives, from the very beginning to the end. He perceives how every event and circumstance interconnects and relates to every other aspect of our lives. In times of uncertainty and challenge, our faith and trust in Him can provide solace and guidance, knowing that He has a master plan that unfolds with divine wisdom and purpose. Trusting in God's knowledge and providence can bring comfort and confidence to our journey through life. Obedience triggers these wonderful attributes of assurance to be released in our lives. And it all commences by listening to His voice.

Throughout this book I have consistently brought to our remembrance the fact that there are consequences to our choices. Choices of commission and choices of omission. Sometimes the latter produces greater consequences. The things we did not do. The promises we ignored. The instructions we failed to heed. The Bible that collected dust. The Scriptures we snubbed. The voice we disregarded. His voice. His personal instructions for our lives.

What Did He Say?

1. **God's Way is Perfect**: Psalm 18:30 reminds us that God's way is perfect, His word is flawless, and He is a shield to those who seek refuge in Him. This underscores the perfection and reliability of God's guidance: *"As for God,* His

way is perfect; the word of the LORD is flawless. He is a shield to all who take refuge *in Him.*" Psalm 18:30

2. **What Seems Right To Us Isn't Necessarily Right**: Proverbs 14:12 warns that what may seem right to us can lead to undesirable outcomes. Our perception versus God's way can be diametrically opposed. My personal example of wanting to continue to teach a Bible Study instead of working for a computer company illustrates the importance of aligning our choices with God's plan rather than relying solely on our own understanding: *"There is a way which seemeth right unto a man, but the end thereof are the ways of death."* Proverbs 14:12 KJV

3. **We Need To Trust His Word Instead Of Trusting Our Own Understanding**: Proverbs 3:5-6 emphasizes the need to trust in the Lord wholeheartedly and not lean solely on our own understanding. Acknowledging God in all our ways allows Him to direct our paths, leading us on the right course. God rewards us for placing our trust in Him. Throughout my life, I've discovered that God acts as a shield, protecting me from my own way and perspective when I place my trust in Him. This happens knowingly and unknowingly in our daily endeavors. He protects me from my OWN way and my OWN perspective. *"Trust in the Lord with all thine heart and lean not on thine own understanding. In all thy ways acknowledge Him and He shall direct thy path."* Proverbs 3:5-6 KJV

The note in the margin of my Bible (August 20, 1980) I referenced in the last chapter, serves as a daily reminder of a lesson learned that continues to impact my life today, highlighting the enduring significance of following God's guidance. God leads us, offering instruction and accompanying promises when we obey. His promises remain eternally true and are fulfilled for those who not only believe but also live out His instructions in their thoughts and actions. His promises are unwavering, provided we not only believe but also act upon His guidance. Unforeseen rewards come from trusting in God's perfect plan and following His direction. Rewards that have been abundantly fulfilling in my life.

The Power of Promises

So why are God's promises so important to us, to our everyday lives? The Book of Romans provides the answer to this question.

> *"In the same way the Spirit comes to help <u>our weakness</u>. <u>We don't know what we should pray</u>, but the Spirit himself pleads our case with unexpressed groans. The one who searches hearts knows how the Spirit thinks, because he pleads for the saints, consistent with God's will. We know that God works all things together for good for the ones who love God, for <u>those who are called</u> according to His purpose.* Romans 8:26-28

Three reasons are identified in this scripture, and all three can be observed in the personal experience shared at the beginning of this chapter.

First, WE ARE WEAK: Our weakness necessitates help, as stated in verse 27: "In the same way, the Spirit comes to help our weakness." When we are weak, we often resort to worrying. And what does God say about worry?

"Therefore, don't worry about tomorrow because tomorrow will worry about itself. Each day has enough trouble of its own." Matthew 6:34

God instructs us to refrain from worrying about tomorrow, as each day has enough troubles of its own. Worrying will not change one thing in our lives. If anything, it only complicates matters more, dumping a bucket of stress into our spirits. Worry dampens our mood and dulls our countenance. Nothing good comes from worry. Remember when God provided manna from heaven for the Children of Israel in the Book of Exodus? He instructed them to collect only enough bread for that day. It was a lesson on trust and provision. If He provided for one day, why wouldn't He provide for the next?

God's faithfulness should continually strengthen us. As we experience God's faithfulness, the promise that He is faithful should empower us with confidence, day by day. Through His strength, we can embrace life's challenges as adventures, rather than dreading them. When we trust in God's promise, our time isn't wasted worrying. We live productive lives living in the PROMISE.

Our part is to first acknowledge our weakness. If we were self-sufficient, we wouldn't need God. The apostle Paul rejoiced in weakness, trials, persecution, and suffering, as he knew God would work it all for his good, demonstrating that he served with God's strength, bringing glory to God, not himself.

Secondly, WE DO NOT KNOW HOW TO PRAY: We need God's promises because we often do not know how to pray effectively. We often pray through a lens of want and self-absorbance. Therefore, God has provided promises for our lives. Specifically, He has promised this:

". . . the Spirit himself pleads our case with unexpressed groans. The one who searches hearts knows how the Spirit thinks, because he pleads for the saints, consistent with God's will." Romans 8:26

Just consider this amazing promise and the powerful truth the promise represents. God provides the Holy Spirit to intercede for us because we really do not know how to pray. The Scripture informs: "the Spirit pleads our case with unexpressed groans, aligning us with God's will. This is a remarkable gift available to us every moment of every day. The Spirit of God is leading us into all truth.

What Did He Say?

"But when He, the Spirit of truth, comes, he will guide you into all the truth. He will not speak on his own; he will speak only what he hears, and he will tell you what is yet to come." John 16:13 NIV

Recounting the story I wrote about earlier in Spokane, during the time when I expected God to shield me, I realized I was mistaken about what I thought I knew. I had no idea what lay ahead in my future, and God was preparing me for a future beyond my wildest dreams.

Thirdly, PREPARATION FOR OUR CALLING: The third reason to believe in God's promises is to prepare us to live out our calling. Preparation should be an integral part of our daily lives. By reading and believing and trusting God's promises, we prepare our lives in advance for what we will experience in reverse.

Most of us understand the concept of preparation in the physical world. We prepare physically for each day after we wake in the morning. If we played sports, we prepared for games through daily practice. We prepare for most physical events in our lives: Meals. Work. Social activities. Vacations. The list is endless. Yet spiritually we often fail in preparation and that's why we easily find ourselves in lands of confusion at various moments in our lives. Confusion that blinds us from seeing God's promises.

Before Jesus sent out the disciples, He first called them to be with Him and to KNOW HIM. He specifically told Peter, "Come follow me and I will make you a fisher of men." He spoke in words a fisher of fish could understand for Peter was a fisherman prior to his encounter with God himself. In the same manner, God speaks to us in a language we understand, a language that's relatable. Do you understand what God is speaking, what He is preparing you for?

Preparation comes in spending time with the Lord in prayer, and in His Word. This shapes us to become more like Him, adopting His heart and thoughts, transforming how we think and live. And it stamps God's promises on our heart, seals them in our spirits.

What Did He Say?

In John 15:7, Jesus emphasizes the importance of abiding in Him and having His words abide in us, enabling us to ask for what we desire in sync with the Spirit's prayers. These prayers are always answered because they align with God's will for us.

> *"If you abide in Me and My words abide in you, you will ask what you desire, and it shall be done for you."* John 15:7

We need promises because of our weakness, our limited understanding, and God's preparation for our calling. Since all of God's promises are personally for us, let's move beyond memorization and live our daily lives consistently with these promises.

CHAPTER 15

IT WAS DURING a significant season of our lives that we learned about God's call into full-time ministry. One Sunday morning at the church we attended, we had the privilege of hosting a missionary who shared a prophetic message with the congregation.

"For the earth will be filled with the knowledge of the glory of the Lord, as the waters cover the sea."
Habakkuk 2:14

When this prophetic word was spoken, both Harley and I immediately sensed that it was directed at us on a personal level. However, at the time, we couldn't fathom how God would use us to spread the knowledge of the Lord to the extent that was prophesied that morning—"as the waters cover the sea." It left us pondering what this meant for a young couple earnestly seeking God's purpose for our lives.

Harley and I were fortunate to be raised by parents who shared a deep belief in global missions work. Even though Harley's mother was a humble widow with limited means, she consistently allocated a portion of her modest income to support missionary endeavors.

My mother held the position of Women's Ministries director at her church, and during that era, Women's Ministries often involved a sewing ministry dedicated to supporting missionaries. The projects frequently centered on crafting items for orphanages and missionary children. Additionally, when missionaries returned home on furlough, my parents graciously hosted them in our home, offering various forms of support and blessings.

As Harley and I embarked on our own ministerial journey, transitioning from Associate Pastor roles to becoming Lead Pastors at First Assembly of God in Spokane and later at Calvary Temple in Concord, we held a deep commitment to missions. This commitment permeated our individual lives, our marriage, and our pastoral leadership.

Building on the relationships we had cultivated with missionaries who had spoken at our churches, we began to receive invitations to teach at their Bible schools or to serve as pastors in international churches while the missionaries were temporarily outside their home countries. These opportunities expanded our understanding of global ministry and deepened our engagement with the worldwide Christian community.

Missionary pastors were often recognized for their impactful crusades, where hundreds and sometimes even thousands of people gathered and embraced Christ as their Lord and Savior. However, our ministry primarily revolved around Bible Schools, where our mission was to equip pastors to effectively lead and nurture local churches in their respective regions. In many of these areas, Bibles were a scarce resource, and there was a significant lack of training available for these local pastors.

The prophetic call to undertake missionary assignments abroad had been spoken over us years earlier, and it was now being realized. Over the course of our ministry journey, we had the privilege of traveling to a remarkable 88 countries, allowing us to witness and contribute to the global expansion of the Christian faith.

And it all started with a word as we were sitting in church. What would have happened if we were hearing but not listening? Or if we dismissed that word as being too general and vague? Or if we failed to diligently pursue that word and be obedient to what God was calling us to do? The trajectory of our lives would be completely different today.

What Did He Say?

"For the earth will be filled with the knowledge of the glory of the Lord, as the waters cover the sea."
Habakkuk 2:14

Now, looking back, we fully grasped the significance of that prophetic word uttered by the missionary many years ago. It was a foretelling that the knowledge of the glory of the Lord would be disseminated across the earth by the very local pastors we were training, equipping them to proclaim Jesus to the ends of the world.

During our extensive travels, we were privileged to experience immense joy in each opportunity we were given to serve. One memorable journey led us to an orphanage in Bucharest, Romania, founded by a single Assembly of God missionary. This missionary had initiated the orphanage for young boys who were homeless and living in the sewers beneath the city.

Upon visiting our church in Concord, she shared a pressing need the orphanage had for shoes. In response, we rallied our congregation, requesting brand new shoes and stockings for boys of specific sizes. The response was overwhelming.

However, when we inquired about shipping the donated shoes, the missionary cautioned that they would likely be stolen and sold on the black market. Instead, she suggested that we personally deliver them.

So, we packed up 13 large moving boxes filled with shoes and embarked on a journey to Romania. Upon arrival, I cleared customs without issue, but Harley encountered a lengthy interrogation. He was questioned about the origin of the shoes and their intended recipients and responding with "I don't know" was deemed insufficient.

Anxious to join me on the other side of customs, Harley eventually convinced the authorities that we were not establishing an illegal shoe operation. However, they claimed that we only had 12 boxes. One of the large boxes had mysteriously disappeared.

Given our limited experience with travel to communist countries, we needed time to navigate this challenging situation. Finally, Harley resorted to offering a $20 bill as an incentive, and within minutes, the missing box was miraculously located. With the 13 boxes in hand, Harley reunited with me.

That day, we delivered the shoes and socks to the children at the orphanage during dinner. It was a heartwarming experience as we personally fitted the right size shoes for each little boy. Witnessing the joy and dancing among those boys was a truly moving moment.

During our stay in Romania, we also visited the underground sewers and saw orphaned children struggling to survive in the harsh winter conditions. Although we desired to distribute shoes to them as well, the missionary wisely advised against it, fearing we would be overwhelmed by people, which could compromise our safety.

Leaving Romania, we departed with a newfound respect and love for missions ministry. Several years later, Harley received an invitation to preach in Romania and serve as the pastor at the Romanian International Church. We left the United States to fulfill this calling and ministered for an entire month.

On our first Sunday at the church, an installation service for a new youth pastor was held. After Harley preached and the service concluded, the new youth pastor approached us, exclaiming, "I know you! You brought shoes to the orphanage where I was raised. Thank you for coming to the orphanage and providing shoes." It was a profound realization that the glory of the Lord was being disseminated through a young orphan boy who had encountered Jesus and later became a voice for the Lord in Romania.

Twice we had the privilege of ministering for a month at the International Church of Romania. Throughout our ministry years, missions remained an integral part of our lives. We embarked on missions journeys that took us to various corners of the globe. These travels allowed us to witness and participate in God's work in diverse regions. Some of the notable destinations we visited during our missions journeys included: Ecuador, Brazil, El Salvador, and Argentina in Central and South America. South Africa, Kenya, Rwanda, and Ethiopia in Africa. Spain, Albania, Portugal, Belgium, Greece, Romania, and Austria in Europe. China, South Korea, India, Vietnam, Myanmar, in Asia. And the Fijian Islands in the South Pacific.

These journeys were opportunities for us to connect with different cultures, share the love of Christ, and contribute to the spread of the Gospel worldwide. Each trip left a lasting impact on our hearts and served as a testament to the power of missions in advancing God's kingdom.

Leading By Example

Missions were not just a part of our ministry but also a significant aspect of our family. It was our custom after dinner each evening for Harley to read a missions-related story to our family, focusing on missionaries and the importance of contributing to missions. As our sons grew, they were presented with opportunities to join mission trips organized by the youth group at our church. During one such mission trip, our eldest son received a call to full-time ministry at the age of 16. This calling eventually materialized after he got married and became a father of two. He and his wife felt compelled to engage in missions work in Mexico.

They, along with their two young boys, relocated to Mexico and began serving God in an orphanage. Our second son pursued a career in medicine and also felt called to engage in medical missions in Mexico. Operating a medical practice in Arizona, he converted a mobile unit into a medical clinic and transported it to Mexico. He was accompanied by a team of medical professionals from his staff in Arizona, as well as his wife and three daughters.

The mobile unit was stationed in the yard of a local church in Mexico, where people sought medical attention. For several years, our son, along with his wife and daughters, offered medical assistance to the Mexican community, while the local pastor shared the Good News of Jesus Christ with those they served. Missions was a part of our heritage and missions was passed along to our boys who shared our love and concern for the work of missions throughout the world.

Looking back, I believe that the essential lesson to glean from the prophetic word spoken by a missionary a decade before we were privileged to experience the reality of that word coming to fruition is this: Whether you receive a word during a Sunday morning sermon, a weekly Bible study, or through a prophetic word spoken to you personally, it is crucial to listen attentively and pray for God to reveal to you how you should prepare for your future.

A Life of Abundance

"The Lord, your Redeemer, the Holy One of Israel says: I am the Lord your God, who teaches you what is good and leads you along the paths you should follow." Isaiah 48:17

The act of listening is fundamental to our relationship with God. He provides guidance, wisdom, and instructions through His word and through the promptings of the Holy Spirit. When we truly listen to His commands and teachings, it's not merely about hearing but about understanding, internalizing, and obeying.

As Isaiah 48:14 emphasizes, God desires that we pay close attention to His commands. It's a way for us to demonstrate our love and devotion to Him. Obedience to God's word is a tangible expression of our faith and trust in Him.

The outcome of our obedience to God's commands indeed has consequences. It shapes our character, influences our actions, and ultimately determines our spiritual journey. By actively listening to and obeying God's guidance, we align our lives with His will and experience the fullness of His blessings. We find life that is unimaginable. A life that is rewarding and fulfilling and overflowing with abundance.

CHAPTER 16

"Be free from pride-filled opinions, for they will only harm your cherished unity. Don't allow self-promotion to hide in your hearts, but in authentic humility put others first and view others as more important than yourselves." Philippians 2:3

THE MARRIAGE RELATIONSHIP is the most significant relationship we will ever experience second only to our relationship with Jesus Christ. It is through our relationship with Christ that we find the guiding principles for our marriages, as illuminated by the Scriptures.

As I pen this chapter on marriage, my husband and I are celebrating 63 glorious years of matrimony. The bedrock of our marital union has undeniably been God's Word, serving as the cornerstone of our relationship.

What Did He Say?

"Then the Lord God said, "It is not good for the man to be alone; I will make him a helper suitable for him." Genesis 2:18

This was the very first lesson God imparted to me about marriage when I encountered the statement in His Word regarding the purpose behind Eve's creation. God declared, "I will make a helper suitable for him." This single scripture provided me with one of the most crucial guidelines for my marriage. It meant that I was to be a suitable helper tailored specifically to my husband's needs. While this directive was broad, I wholeheartedly endeavored to be an appropriate partner for him.

Later, the verse in Philippians 2:3, as mentioned above, served as another source of instruction for me. Consequently, I had two distinct lessons from God's Word on how to be a wife to my husband. Firstly, my attitude and behavior should be in harmony with the man I married, and secondly, I was to prioritize my husband's needs and desires over my own. I recognized that there was work to be done.

Since being self-centered is innate from birth, it isn't easy to let go of self. Observing young children is a vivid illustration of the inherent self-focused nature of our minds, wills, and emotions. One of the earliest words children often learn to say is "mine!" The prevalence of self-centered behavior is evident in mankind from birth. However, transformation from this behavior can only be achieved through the rebirth that Jesus provided for us on the cross.

So, what does "self" entail?

1. Your individual character or behavior
2. The combined elements of one's body, mind, and emotions
3. Your entire person

Steps to Change

When we are uncertain about events and circumstances in life, when we need direction and answers, we must go to the source of all wisdom to find answers: God's Word. So that is where I started. My search of the scriptures on the topic of marriage, seeking how I could change to become a better partner and have a great marriage led to four steps:

Step One

I Corinthians 13:11 *"When I was a child, I spoke as a child, I understood as a child, I thought as a child: but when I became a man (woman), I put away childish things." (KJV).*

This was indeed an aspect of "self" that demanded significant transformation in my life. Thanks to the guidance provided in the above verse, I was acutely aware of the specific facet I needed to address: my emotions. And address them I did. The journey of embracing this change was substantial. Drawing insights from scripture, I discerned the steps I needed to take. I subsequently sought God's assistance, and He readily extended His help. I made the conscious choice to put away childish behaviors. Here, too, the scriptures remained my steadfast guide.

Step Two

"But now God has set the members, each one of them, in the body just as He pleased. And if they were all one member, where would the body be. But now indeed there are many members, yet one body." 1 Cor. 12:18-20

This scripture illuminated a profound truth for me: that within the marriage relationship, God had bestowed unique gifts upon each of us, and that these gifts held equal significance. In fact, our differences served to enrich our marriage.

These distinctive gifts provided us with distinct perspectives on life. It became evident to me that my perspective, shaped by my own gifting, was just as valuable as my husband's. This realization was an eye-opener; it underscored the fact that there wasn't a singular "right" perspective. Instead, both perspectives were equally valid, albeit different. Interestingly, I also recognized the importance of conveying this lesson to my husband.

Our decision-making process evolved into a mutual learning experience, marked by a genuine appreciation for each other's opinions and perspectives. Through this collaborative process, we learned from each other and arrived at solutions that harmonized both perspectives and were mutually agreeable. Change was indeed necessary, and it happened.

Step Three

"His divine power has granted to us all things that pertain to life and godliness, through the knowledge of him who called us to his own glory and excellence..." 2 Peter 1:3 ESV

The ability to know God grants us access to the truth concerning all aspects of life and godliness—an incredible gift indeed. We need not stumble through married life in the dark; He illuminates our path. There is no need to wander in confusion and failure and misery in marriage. We can find fulfillment and abundance.

God's Word serves as a guiding light for anyone desiring to follow His instructions. These instructions are not intricate; they are accessible to all. The challenge arises when we must decide whether to heed these instructions or disregard them, opting instead to forge our own path.

The Book of Proverbs grants incredible insight into marriage and relationships and offers profound wisdom. In Proverbs 14:12, we read these words: "There is a way that seems right to a man, but the end thereof leads to destruction." This truth raises a crucial question: Why would we follow what appears right to us when it goes against God's instructions? The reality is that such a choice ultimately leads to destruction. Destruction in various aspects of life and in our marriages.

Step Four

"Jesus once again addressed them: "I am the world's Light. No one who follows me stumbles around in the darkness. I provide plenty of light to live in." John 8:12

The scriptures serve as our life manual. Why wander in darkness when we can confidently walk in the light, secure in the knowledge that by living in obedience to God's Word, our marriage will flourish, bringing true life to ourselves, our spouses, and our children?

Regular self-examination should be an integral part of our lives. Ask yourself, how have I transformed since accepting Christ? If you're married, reflect on how your marriage has evolved due to the guidance found in the Bible, our life manual. Embracing change becomes essential if we aim to relinquish self-centeredness and prioritize others over ourselves, including our spouses.

Recognize that "self" encompasses our physical, mental, and emotional aspects. Let's explore each of these facets individually, considering how we can shed behaviors that tarnish our character and cultivate behaviors that nurture it.

"I have been crucified with Christ, and I no longer live, but Christ lives in me. And the life that I now live in my body, I live by faith, indeed by the faithfulness of God's Son, who loved me and gave himself for me." Galatians 2:20

Paul's life serves as a remarkable example for us all. He reached a point where he could confidently declare, "I no longer live; I have died to self," and he allowed Christ to take center stage in his life. His existence became intertwined with the life of Christ, shaping his behavior and actions. The profound declaration of having died to self is truly inspiring, as it underscores the transformation that occurs when Christ resides within us, guiding our conduct.

As Christians, we must recognize that our bodies serve as the temple of the Holy Spirit. Our minds house the Spirit, and aligning our emotions with the Spirit requires self-denial.

God has provided us with the opportunity to live in this manner, experiencing the abundant life He has prepared for us on Earth and in eternity in Heaven. The scriptures offer comprehensive guidance, including instructions for the marriage relationship. No aspect of life is left unaddressed.

Paul's epistle to the Ephesian church contains explicit instructions for both husbands and wives. These guidelines are straightforward and easily comprehensible. When put into practice, they yield remarkable and transformative results within the marriage relationship. Here is what he writes for husbands and wives:

> *"For wives, this means being devoted to your husbands like you are tenderly devoted to our Lord, for the husband provides leadership for the wife, just as Christ provides leadership for his church, as the Savior and Reviver of the body. In the same way the church is devoted to Christ, let wives be devoted to the husbands in everything."* Ephesians 5:22 (PASSION)

> *"And to the husbands, you are to demonstrate love for your wives with the same tender devotion that Christ demonstrated to us, his bride. Husbands*

have the obligation of loving and caring for their wives the same way they love and care of their own bodies, for to love your wife is to love your own self. No one abuses his own body but pampers it — serving and satisfying its needs. That's exactly what Christ does for his church!" Ephesians 5:25,28-29 (PASSION)

I've experienced sixty-three wonderful years of marriage? It's no surprise that my love for God's Word runs deep. I've chosen to follow God's instructions for my marriage. Embracing and living by the truth serves as the foundation for success in every facet of life. Through my journey as a supportive partner to my husband, I've been blessed with numerous opportunities to apply my unique gifts and calling. These opportunities were made possible solely because of my role as Harley's wife. Obedience to God's Word has yielded remarkable dividends in my life.

What Did He Say?

"Seek first the kingdom of God and His righteousness and all these things shall be added unto you," Matthew 6:33

APPENDIX: A WORD FOR MOTHERS

❧

THE BIBLE PROVIDES us with numerous examples of parenting styles and choices made by people with their children. These examples offer valuable insights as we observe the consequences of their parenting decisions. I've personally gleaned many lessons from the stories of biblical mothers, and I hope you will too.

In this appendix, we'll uncover profound truths through the story of Jocabed, a mother who gave birth to Moses, the future deliverer of Israel from Egyptian bondage. Her story illuminates how to navigate crises effectively.

To make this information applicable to your life, please consider how the story of this biblical character relates to your own circumstances. By personalizing the Scriptures and exploring their relevance to your life, the Bible transforms from a mere storybook into a life manual.

As I delved into Moses's story, one aspect that stood out was his mother, Jocabed. Her remarkable response to an unimaginable crisis in her family's life left a lasting impression on me. Her defining characteristic was her faith, and it profoundly influenced her approach to the crisis.

Jocabed faced a dire situation involving her newborn son, Moses. Pharaoh had decreed that all firstborn male Hebrew babies be thrown into the Nile to curb the Israelites' growing population. Many Hebrew women responded to this crisis with fear, leading them to follow the decree and sacrifice their infants to the river. However, Jocabed chose a different path, driven by faith, which not only saved her son but also paved the way for his destiny as the deliverer of Israel.

I want to highlight three essential qualities that mothers should embrace:

1) Creativity: Recognize that we are created in God's image, imbued with creative abilities. Like Jocabed, we can employ our creativity to find solutions to family crises. Jocabed complied with Pharaoh's edict but driven by faith, found a way to save her baby's life through a cleverly constructed basket, thereby transforming a potential tragedy into a triumph.

2) Observant: Faith allows us to make practical observations in challenging situations. Jocabed hid her baby for three months and during this time, keenly observed the habits of the Pharaoh's daughter, the ideal spot to place Moses in the Nile, and the optimal moment to do so. Timing plays a critical role in crisis management, and faith equips us to make timely observations.

3) Develop a Plan: Over the course of those three months, Jocabed formulated a plan. She designated Moses's older sister to place him in the river, with instructions to watch over him. When the Pharaoh's daughter discovered Moses,

his sister cleverly suggested that a Hebrew mother nurse the baby, a plan the Pharaoh's daughter embraced. This creative, observant, and well-thought-out plan allowed Jocabed to nurse her own child and receive compensation for it. Her faith in action turned a crisis into an opportunity.

I share this story because it personally resonates with me. Years ago, my 15-year-old daughter ran away from home and returned at 16, six months pregnant. My husband and I were pastors at the time, facing a daunting crisis. We had to decide whether to respond in fear, advocating for abortion, or in faith, seeking a solution. We chose faith and had three months to find a creative, observant, and well-devised plan to ensure our grandchild's life and future.

We discovered an adoption agency that offered classes for expectant teenage girls, helping them decide whether to raise their babies or choose adoption. Our daughter completed the course, and by the end, she had made her decision, guided by wisdom and concern for her baby's welfare. Like Jocabed, we entrusted our grandchild to another family, knowing it was the right choice for his destiny.

Moses was a child of destiny, chosen to be a deliverer. I firmly believe that all children are children of destiny. Even our grandchild, raised in his adoptive home, was part of God's plan for his life. Faith plays a pivotal role in our lives as women, whether we are mothers or face different challenges like health or finances. In every difficult situation, we have a choice: faith, which empowers us to be creative, observant, and planful, or fearful.

In conclusion, I want to emphasize the profound influence you have on your children. When you make wise choices and live a life of faith like Jocabed, your children witness the benefits of your lifestyle and are more likely to choose the path of faith. Hebrews

11:23 and 11:27 highlight the significance of faith in Moses's life and its impact on those around him.

A mother who lives without fear produces children who fear not. The way you handle crises shapes the lives of those you influence. Will your loved ones be guided by your faith, expressed through creativity, observance, and thoughtful planning? I pray that this lesson from Moses's mother inspires and encourages you to be a person of faith, regardless of your circumstances. Now, you know what to do!

Printed in the USA
CPSIA information can be obtained
at www.ICGtesting.com
CBHW062120201223
2756CB00007BA/155

9 781662 888564